Ineffable
LöVE

Ineffable LoVE

Exploring Christian themes in
GOOD OMENS
A study guide based on the hit TV series

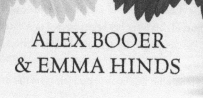

ALEX BOOER
& EMMA HINDS

DARTON · LONGMAN + TODD

First published as an eBook in 2020 by
Darton, Longman and Todd Ltd
1 Spencer Court
140 – 142 Wandsworth High Street
London SW18 4JJ

First published in paperback 2022.

ISBN 978-0-232-53454-2

A catalogue record for this book is available from the British Library

Designed and produced by Judy Linard

Printed and bound by Ashford Colour Press, Gosport

Contents

Introduction

'It's Ineffable. It is beyond understanding and incapable of
being put into words.'
Good Omens

'No one can comprehend what goes on under the sun.
Despite all their efforts to search it out, no one can discover
its meaning. Even if the wise claim they know,
they cannot really comprehend it.'
Ecclesiastes 8:17

God loves the world, according to the Gospel of John (3:16). So much, in fact, that the Word that was God, that was present In the Beginning, became human in body and joined us in solidarity on Earth (John 1:14). This is how the story of Jesus begins: with incarnation in an unjust world. Though we face fear and our own failures, we have hope that in the presence of death we find new life triumphant through love.

The Christian faith invites us to dwell on these themes and embody in our own lives the journey of sacrifice, death and rebirth, which is the aim of the readings and discussion guides in this book. It aims to encourage us to explore the themes of our faith and invite God to interrupt us, to break us and let us regrow anew.

On the face of it, the television adaptation of *Good Omens* seems an odd starter for Christian reflection. It began life as a parody of American cult horror film *The Omen*, as a book by authors Neil Gaiman and Terry Pratchett, published in 1990, born out of the premise, 'What if William Brown, of Richmal Crompton's *Just William*, was the Antichrist?'. Before Terry Pratchett died in 2015 of early-onset Alzheimer's, Neil Gaiman had promised him that he would realise their long-held plans to make an adaptation for the screen. *Good Omens* the TV show aired in May 2019. The TV show, then, is a story about love, made with love, as a love letter to a dead friend. The care and attention to detail, as well as the affection invested by those involved, is reflected in every frame.

The story follows an angel, Aziraphale, and a demon, Crowley, who are under-cover representatives on Earth of Heaven and Hell respectively. They are disheartened to discover their managerial superiors in Heaven and Hell are keen to bring about the long-anticipated Apocalypse, the Last Battle and the End of the World. Crowley and Aziraphale have become rather comfortable on Earth (Aziraphale owns an antiquarian bookshop, Crowley drives a vintage Bentley and keeps house-plants) and they don't feel any inclination to let it be destroyed. Finding themselves on common ground, though nominally on opposing sides of the conflict, they work together to thwart the plan to bring about Armageddon through the coming of the Antichrist – who is, in this case, a rather thoughtful English boy who has no idea he's a pawn in a game with ultimate consequences. Chaos unfolds, love blooms, loyalties are tested and unlikely alliances are forged between all manner of supernatural and human beings who are alike only in desiring kindness, compassion and a continued opportunity to rejoice in the absurd and infinite variety of God's creation. Together, they fight to prevail over the approaching disaster of Armageddon: an ego-driven contest of dominance between Heaven and Hell that will destroy all of humanity.

In some ways, a Christian interpretation of *Good Omens* seems redundant. Much of the story uses a broadly Christian-adjacent mythology – and we mean mythology, rather than theology – as its playground. On a superficial level, therefore, it's easy to point and say something like, 'Look, this bit is a bit like Jesus!' especially when it's the bit with Jesus in it. The story begins in the beginning* and ends with a new beginning, initiated by the birth of a child and ushered in by his sacrifice as he lays down his power and submits to earthly limitations and his father's authority, turning the established order on its head to save humanity and renew all of creation. In the new world, lions lie down with lambs – strictly metaphorically. Enemies dine together and strangers are brought together as family. No doubt all involved in the show's production are fully aware of the parallels.

Perhaps it's even more easy to become affronted and

---

* ... a very good place to start.

cry, 'But God/the angels/the demons would never do that!' when Jon Hamm's besuited Archangel Gabriel is flaunting his particular brand of managerial intimidation or using language unbecoming of an authority figure addressing their subordinate. Or when the demon Crowley is interceding with God on behalf of humanity. That said, while the show is woven through with Biblical references, it mostly adopts its tropes from Dante, Milton and the 1970s/80s craze for pseudo-biblical dispensationalist apocalyptica, as typified by the work of Hal Lindsey, rather than from orthodox schools of theology. This book does not claim any versions of *Good Omens* to be a literal interpretation of history or of Christian theology, and we certainly don't read it as a template for what is or isn't 'real'. It's the story that's the important thing.

We have attempted to draw out the themes and the narrative arc of the show because they resonate so strongly with the themes of our faith. The apocalyptic window-dressing is almost incidental. It's really hard to avoid the fact that the fundamentals of the story are incredibly Jesus-y.

In substance, the story is about the frustrations of longing for justice in an unjust world and what it means to be Good or Bad, Right or Wrong. It's about the choices we all have to make to move through this world, and it asks of us the question: What is it that saves us? Like much of Jesus' teaching, this story is subversive and challenging. It's gentle, loving and concerned with creation and good caretaking. It has much to say about the nature of power and the corruption of institutions and who is and isn't blessed. This is a story in which love with the courage to transgress traditional boundaries leads to life. Self-acceptance, truth – acknowledging 'reality, angel' – and sacrifice for the sake of others save the world. In the end, it's about hope, redemption and renewal.

God knows we need those things. When we wrote this book, back in 2019, we drew attention to what we saw as the challenges of our time: the urgent climate crisis, global political instability, personal insecurity, and an increasing hatred toward minorities of all kinds. Now we must add a new global pandemic to this list, which seems to have only exacerbated the original circumstances and brought the inequalities of people's experiences into sharper relief. We are desperate to find a way through. We always need new ways to explore our own story and the way of Jesus.

HOW TO USE THIS BOOK

We hope you feel free to use this book however you like! However, we have assumed that you'll have seen all six episodes of the *Good Omens* TV series before you start. Spoilers therefore abound throughout! What we have to say probably won't make a lot of sense without the context of the TV show. This even goes for those who've read the book or listened to the BBC radio show: while the fundamentals of the story are the same, there are several new characters and emotional arcs in the TV show that aren't introduced in the other versions.

We've written this book with individual study in mind, but it would be easy enough to adapt it to a group format if that suits you. It's divided into six chapters, which could be adapted to a six-week course or discussion group in whatever manner you deem to be most appropriate and inclusive for your own community.

We hope you enjoy the process however you choose to use this book and that you're challenged, encouraged, inspired, amused and moved as we were in writing it. However you feel about your own viewing experience, we hope there's something here for us, as the church, to meditate on and rejoice in as we explore our faith.

USING THIS BOOK CREATIVELY

Good Omens has had a significant impact on popular culture since it aired and a second season has been announced. When creating our guide, we felt it important to acknowledge this impact in a way fitting to the show, and so each study is accompanied by a 'Get Creative' section at the end. This is an opportunity for you to creatively engage with Good Omens like so many have been doing worldwide. We've also shared our own creative reflections!

There has been an outpouring of fan creativity, discussion and interpretation in the last few months, mostly expressed online. It's been a kind of festival of joy that so far hasn't shown a sign of slowing down. Transformative Works[2] – mostly stories and art, but also songs, toys, essays and poetry – are being made and passed around the world with cheerful abandon. Fans have been using the inspiration of Good Omens to shine new light on their own experience, or their observations of the world around them, or their own theology, philosophies and ethical conflicts. Which is of course also what we're doing here.

This book of ours can't hope to top some of the truly creative examples so far. There have been fan conventions, books of art, jewellery, dolls, online comics, tattoos, you name it. Of particular note is the clay tablet inscribed with Neo-Assyrian Cuneiform 'found' by a researcher into dead languages. When translated, it is revealed to be a letter addressed to 'Azirapil' from a 'Crawly.'[3]

Not all fanworks are this spectacular. Alex likes to write stories, but her housemate Rachael has been making poseable crochet models of Aziraphale and Crowley. These now appear throughout the house, waving to us from the top of the microwave or having picnics on the bookshelves.

We'd like to encourage you to contribute your own creative expression and have included a story prompt in the 'Get Creative' section that will set you off into the world of fan creation! We do hope you'll share your art and stories with us or the wider fandom if you feel so inclined – #GoodOmens on social media – or please do share with us your own transformative works. You can find us on Twitter @IneffablyLovely

Opening prayer

If you'll allow us, we'd like to cheerfully pray for you, our readers:

> May you find within yourself the power and joy of your own imagination;
> A holy anger at injustice;
> Peace in your body, Comfort in your grief.
> May you have hope for the future;
> Wisdom in your relationships;
> A great love for the world.
> May you laugh, and delight in the unknowable yet intimate absurdity of God.

A NOTE ON PRONOUNS

God is neither male nor female, a trait – according to both book and TV canon – they share with all the angels and demons in Good Omens and one of the horsepersons of the apocalypse.[4]

Good Omens the book uses male pronouns for God. The TV show, in which She is our omniscient narrator, generally uses female ones, although Jesus addresses Him as Father from the cross. We could also use the gender neutral They, not least because it conveniently represents both singular and plural and therefore encompasses the Trinity in all its confusing glory. We're going to be deliberately inconsistent throughout this book and use all three options, in reflection of the range of genders represented in the *Good Omens* TV show and, increasingly, in our congregations.

As well as binary trans men and women (people whose gender is in some way different to that assigned at their birth[5]), in *Good Omens* there are least two main characters whose gender isn't binary at all: Crowley (whose gender is portrayed as fluid) and Pollution, whose pronouns are they/them.

We've attached an appendix about welcoming non-binary people and using them/they pronouns at the back of this book.

✪ ✪ ✪

Note on Bible translations: Unless otherwise specified, we have adopted the New International Version when quoting the Bible.

CHAPTER ONE
Justice: Like a River

'You could say to the universe, this is not fair. And the
universe would say: Oh, isn't it? Sorry.'
Terry Pratchett, *Soul Music*

'We know that the whole creation has been groaning as in
the pains of childbirth right up to the present time.'
Romans 8:22

BIBLE READING
Genesis 18:16–33. Abraham bargains for Sodom

TO START YOU THINKING
Alex's maternal grandmother used to express disappointment with a very British tut and a head shake of disapproval. She was also devoted to her garden and the natural world – except for slugs, to which she showed no mercy. 'This is how we deal with slugs, children,' she'd tell us, while she lined the poor unfortunate things up on the concrete flags and split them in two with one blow of the garden spade.

Aziraphale-as-Brother-Francis would frown on this heinous treatment of Sister Slug, but I suspect he was a rather terrible gardener.

Alongside slugs, Grandma's tut would mostly be deployed for things that were Not Fair. She'd watch the Six O'clock News, listen to reports on famines overseas, new wars and old, preventable environmental disasters and news of people gone before their time, shake her head, tut and say, 'It's not *right.*'

We think most of us want things to be fair, at least in our favour if not across the board. A desire for things to be made right is a thread that runs solidly through the Bible and the ache is palpable throughout the words of the psalmists, the prophets and the poets.

The Psalms have various takes on God's justice and whether or not the world is fair. Some, such as Psalm 1, seem to suggest – like Aziraphale – that the righteous prosper and 'wickedness contains the seeds of its own destruction'. Like Crowley, we're inclined to respond sceptically. Where on

Earth have they *been*? It certainly doesn't seem like they're paying attention to the world we're experiencing. Perhaps the Psalm is aspirational or prophetic.

More typically, the psalmists use their songs to lament and to long for justice that they don't yet see, or to petition God to save them from unfairness. The psalmists are convinced that God, like them, is not content for wickedness to prosper. We sense that justice and a fair balance of power is a right thing to want, and yet we know we don't have it.

All creation groans. It's not fair. It's not right.

As in the Biblical narratives, the characters in *Good Omens* wrestle with these matters and in doing so invite us to wrestle along with them. The moral heart of the mini-series is the demon Crowley, an imperfect but sincere prophet who looks at the world and is unafraid to challenge our assumptions about Good and Bad, Right and Wrong and whether fairness has any kind of a say in all this.

His well-meaning counterpart Aziraphale, in contrast, hopes it'll all be sorted out through common sense and trusts in the reigning authorities. Surely someone sensible is in charge and they've got this all in hand? But a quick look at the news in our world on any given day would suggest Aziraphale's hope is a futile one. It's a shallow and naive expectation, predicated on trust in a system that's really set up to serve itself rather than concern itself with those hurt by its agenda. It takes Aziraphale over 6000 years to realise that not everyone has his pure intentions.

Crowley, though, is the boy calling out the emperor on his nakedness. He stands next to Noah's Ark – a story we cheerfully share with children! – and asks why God decided the children of the time deserve to die. 'Sounds more like something our lot would do', he says, appalled. What sort of God plans this?

Much later, Crowley prays to God and begs to understand Her Great Plan, asking her to have mercy on humanity.

Jesus, in his great manifesto portrayed in the Beatitudes (Matthew 5:3–10), announced that those who notice the world's unfairness and long for righteousness are blessed.

'Blessed are the poor in spirit,
  for theirs is the kingdom of heaven.
Blessed are those who mourn,
  for they will be comforted.
Blessed are the meek,
  for they will inherit the earth.
Blessed are those who hunger and thirst for righteousness,
  for they will be filled.

Blessed are the merciful,
  for they will be shown mercy.
Blessed are the pure in heart,
  for they will see God.
Blessed are the peacemakers,
  for they will be called children of God.
Blessed are those who are persecuted because of righteousness,
  for theirs is the kingdom of heaven.'

It's still our hope.

Alex's grandmother lived a faithful life, served her church, her community, and her family and seemingly never wavered in her fundamental belief that there was right and there was wrong and that there was such a thing as justice, even if she didn't see it play out in the world around us.

The way of Jesus – of sacrifice, death and rebirth – offers Christianity's hope for the future and also hope for justice now in the coming of what the Gospel of Matthew calls the Kingdom of Heaven. This idea of 'now and not yet,' the recognition that while all creation certainly groans, our hope for the future doesn't mean we sit on our hands and watch the seas boil and dolphins turn to bouillon, but insists that we get on with it and do what it is we judge to be right. Jesus challenges us to examine our hearts, ask ourselves difficult questions and, where we see ourselves headed down a path of unrighteousness, to repent – or 'turn around' – and take action.

In this chapter we explore God's plan; right and wrong; what faithfulness means; and what it is to long for righteousness, to make peace, to take responsibility and make choices that ensure we do our best to preserve the Earth for the meek (and the slugs) to inherit. We'll consider Crowley and his longing for mercy, and the character that probably demonstrates the most faithfulness in the show, the International Express Delivery Driver!

Prayer [1]

We bring these names before the Almighty.
We cry: Justice.

Ellie Gould, 17 years old. A British teenager murdered by a 17-year-old boy.
We cry: Justice.

Alex Milkovich, 19 years old. A Russian man murdered for being transgender.
We cry: Justice.

Oscar Grant, 22 years old. A young black man murdered by police.
We cry: Justice.

The injustice of this world burns us. We come to the cross for healing, and we cry.
Justice.
Amen.

STARTING QUESTION

Emma asks:

When I was a child, my siblings and I played board games. It was generally traumatic for all of us, as my sister loved to cheat and my brother had a profound sense of childhood justice. Whenever he caught her with extra monopoly money in her sock or taking a quick peek in Cluedo, he would start a fight of epic proportions, necessarily including loud shrieks of: 'It's not right! It's NOT FAIR!'

We all have memories of times in our lives when, like my brother, we knew something was definitely Not Fair. Do you have a specific childhood memory of when you felt something was very unfair? How do you feel fairness develops inside us?

WATCH: ON THE GARDEN WALL

Garden scene – The Ineffable Plan (Episode 1, 2:23 to 6:20)
The Angel of the Eastern Gate and the Serpent of Eden chat about Right and Wrong as they watch Adam and Eve make their way out of the Garden, carrying a flaming sword gifted to them by the angel. They are a little worried that they may have done their jobs rather badly. The demon Crowley (currently going by the name Crawly) ponders the whole thing with questions and puzzled commentary, while Aziraphale voices the opinion that it's best not to speculate. Indeed, he thinks it's Ineffable – or beyond understanding, incapable of definition. According to Aziraphale, Right and Wrong are constants, as specified by the Almighty, and transgressions from the rules deserve to be punished. Neither of them seems particularly convinced by this. Crowley notices that Aziraphale is missing his sword and finds out that, when faced with obeying orders versus the opportunity to give humanity a fighting chance, Aziraphale has in fact erred on the side of compassion rather than the rules. Crowley jokes perhaps they both got it wrong; he thinks it's amusing. Aziraphale continues to fret. Atop the

wall surrounding the Garden, Aziraphale shelters Crowley from the first rains under one outstretched wing.

PROMPT QUESTIONS

1. In this scene, we see the Fall of Humanity and watch Adam and Eve leave the Garden. How do you feel about the representation of Eden in this scene? Crowley wonders whether God intended it to be this way all along. What do you think? Did God plan the fall?

2. Aziraphale seems initially to believe that Right and Wrong are clear cut and a matter of specific rules, but his very first actions on the mortal plane suggest his instincts are that it's more complicated. What do you make of Aziraphale's decision to trust his judgement rather than prioritising his orders?

3. Throughout the series, we see that God has some unlikely characters to carry out Her Ineffable Plans. In our reality, how do you see God's plan working in the world? Who is involved in that plan? Do you have any examples from your own experience?

GOING DEEPER
But Why?

> 'People were bringing little children to Jesus for him to place his hands on them, but the disciples rebuked them. When Jesus saw this, he was indignant. He said to them, 'Let the little children come to me, and do not hinder them, for the kingdom of God belongs to such as these. Truly I tell you, anyone who will not receive the kingdom of God like a little child will never enter it.' And he took the children in his arms, placed his hands on them and blessed them.' (Mark 10:13–16)

In 2016, the world sadly lost one of its icons of screen and film, the incomparable Gene Wilder. Beloved by many for his various roles, he shall only ever occupy one role in the heart of children born in the eighties: Willy Wonka from *Willy Wonka and the Chocolate Factory*. Wilder put his own quirks and wonder into the role to create the effervescent yet prickly chocolatier and one of the best things about him was the way he responded to questions. Often with an inane rhyme, ('Oh, you should never ever doubt what nobody is sure about,') or a sarcastic comment, ('I'm sorry but all questions must be submitted in writing,') but most often a swift backfire of another question. When asked by the genuinely terrible Mr Beauregarde, 'What is this, Wonka, some kind of fun house?' he responds, 'Why? Are you having fun?' There is something of the child in Willy Wonka, with his love of candy, his delight in mischief, and most importantly, his penchant for difficult questions.

When we read Mark's account of the little children, it's hard not to imagine the noise. A gaggle of excitable children pressing in from all sides, questions brimming on their lips. This moment in Jesus' ministry comes at the height of his popularity, when crowds of people were travelling the countryside to listen to him teach. There must have been many children in that mix of Galileans, Judeans, and Samaritans but this is the first time they are brought into the text. In the verses prior to this in Mark's narrative, he is met by Pharisees who wrestle with Jesus' teaching by questioning it. This was entirely expected. Jesus and the Pharisees come from a culture where God and His will are sought by asking questions, so there was no need for the disciples to try and protect their Master from their thoughts. However, a throng of sticky children was clearly another matter. Yet, in the Torah, it is specified that not only will children ask questions of their teachers, but that it is the duty of the wise to enable them and also give answers where they can. (Exodus 12:26–27, Exodus 13:14, Deuteronomy 6:20–21). In addition to these prophecies of curious children, the people of Abraham follow their patriarch's lead in establishing a faith built on questions. 'Why, O Lord, have you brought trouble on these people?' Moses asks; 'Why does the wicked way prosper?' questions Jeremiah. Jesus knew the value of a questioning child. His own, last human breath contained the vital, heart-rent question of a desperate child to their parent: 'My God, my God, why have you forsaken me?' This is interesting in the context of *Good Omens* because although Crowley gives several excuses as to why he fell from heaven throughout the show, in his most vulnerable moment of confession, alone in his flat and crying out to God, he claims, 'I only ever asked questions. That's all it took to become a demon in the old days.'

Do you think God rejects us for asking questions? Do you put limits on the questions you ask God? If so, what questions do you think are over the line? Why?

Like Crowley, our childlike questions of faith often speak to our most vulnerable and urgent concerns. They often have a way of cutting to the heart of the matter. Author and preacher Sarah Bessey, in her 2015 book *Out of Sorts* draws attention to the ways of her own little children and their questions inform how she understands this moment in Mark 10. She says:

> There is a natural curiosity that is inherent to children. I think it's a bit dishonest to use, 'Have faith like a child' as a way to shut a person down. Like, somehow, it means we're not supposed to wonder, we're just supposed to accept. Now that I have a house full of small humanity, I think I'm beginning to understand why Jesus would encourage us to have faith like a child. They don't know. And so they ask.[2]

'God, are you listening?' asks Crowley, who certainly whines like a toddler. With his next breath (do demons breathe?) he begins to plead directly with God, as a child might plead for just five more minutes before bed, on behalf of humanity:

'Okay, I know. You're testing them, you said you were going to be testing them. But you shouldn't test them to destruction. Not to the end of the world.' As with Abraham in our earlier reading, the act of questioning seems to facilitate intimacy with God rather than create separation. Is Crowley, like Jesus suggested, coming closer to God by being childlike? How do you think God answers Crowley's prayer?

Aziraphale also tries to intercede on Earth's behalf. He goes about it rather differently: instead of questioning, a concept which Aziraphale seems to balk from throughout the show, he attempts to make contact through the heavenly hierarchy and management system. He approaches Gabriel and the other Archangels, and what has up until this point been polite but quietly frantic enquiry, does finally become a similar childlike tantrum to Crowley. 'You, you're... Bad Angels!' Aziraphale tearfully spits out, as if this gentle expletive is the worst curse he could think of. Taking his plea to 'a higher authority,' the palms of his hands pressed together in a parody of a child's prayer, Aziraphale never manages to speak directly with God. His despair as he accepts the reality of Heaven's bureaucratic denial ('The point is not to avoid the war, but to win it!') is palpable in his expression.

We all come to moments in life where the fluency of our daily thought is struck mute by life. All we might be left with is the small, childlike voice asking over and over again: 'Why?'

FOLLOW UP QUESTIONS

- What do you think of the ways that these two characters try to approach God?
- Do you see different branches of Christianity represented in their approaches?
- Do you see yourself in either of them? Draw from your own prayer habits or aspirations, if you're using this in a group setting and if you're comfortable sharing.

WATCH: THE SUMMONING OF WAR
(Episode 2: 3:58 – 6:34)

Our Divine Narrator informs us the summoning of the Four Horsemen of the Apocalypse has been outsourced to the International Express Company, whose delivery driver pulls up to a town in disputed territory in North Africa. Nearby, peace negotiations are interrupted by a smirking red-haired woman. She's supremely unbothered by the raised guns and aggressive warnings of various guards. The representatives of each faction turn to sign the formal accord but petty arguments break out over the pen, which rapidly devolve into vicious accusations and an armed standoff. The International Express Man arrives on the scene, makes awkward small talk and hands over a parcel to the woman. She unwraps a sword and breathes, 'Finally.' As she makes her excuses and swaggers off, gunfire breaks out in the tent behind her and engulfs the town as she strides through the streets. 'This is War', says God, and her busy work on Earth, 'Killing time and, sometimes, people', is coming to an end – along with the world.

PROMPT QUESTIONS

1. War incites a massacre without lifting a finger. How does she do this?

2. Can you identify the emotions and particular fears of the participants of the peace treaty? How do we see these emotions and fears enacted in the real world?

3. As demonstrated by his actions and his clipboard, the International Express Man has a clearly defined To-Do List. We never see where his instructions come from. What is his part in the divine plan?

GOING DEEPER
Does God plan violence?
Emma reflects:

Revelation 6:1–8

'I watched as the Lamb opened the first of the seven seals. Then I heard one of the four living creatures say in a voice like thunder, 'Come!' I looked, and there before me was a white horse! Its rider held a bow, and he was given a crown, and he rode out as a conqueror bent on conquest.

When the Lamb opened the second seal, I heard the second living creature say, 'Come!' Then another horse came out, a fiery red one. Its rider was given power to take peace from the earth and to make people kill each other. To him was given a large sword.

When the Lamb opened the third seal, I heard the third living creature say, 'Come!' I looked, and there before me was a black horse! Its rider was holding a pair of scales in his hand. Then I heard what sounded like a voice among the four living creatures, saying, 'Two pounds of wheat for a day's wages, and six pounds of barley for a day's wages, and do not damage the oil and the wine!'

When the Lamb opened the fourth seal, I heard the voice of the fourth living creature say, 'Come!' I looked, and there before me was a pale horse! Its rider was named Death, and Hades was following close behind him. They were given power over a fourth of the earth to kill by sword, famine and plague, and by the wild beasts of the earth.'

I recall the first introduction I had to militarised language in the church. It was in a school hall, aged seven, part of a large congregation of children with unfortunate drums and instruments, banging away to 'Marching in the light of God.' A Christian classic, I must have sung it as part of many tuneless children's choruses over a hundred times in my childhood. It is only as an adult that I consider the oddness of it as a Sunday school favourite. It does not teach of God's creation or the person of Jesus Christ like the much-beloved 'If I was a butterfly.' It is a song with roots in opposition and political protest. Translated from the South African song 'Siyahamba,' this song was first popularised worldwide in the 1984 songbook, *Freedom is Coming: Songs of Protest and Praise from South Africa*. A strange choice then, for a children's band in rural southern England. Yet so many of our worship songs include language associated with militarisation, and in its own turn, violence.

When the four Horsepeople make their gradual appearance in *Good Omens* we understand them in a certain context: Doom. They are an inevitable part of the march towards Armageddon. Even if their actual summoning isn't the Archangel Gabriel's department, it's 'All going according to the Divine Plan. The hell hound has been set loose and now the four horsemen of the Apocalypse are being summoned: Death, Pollution, Famine, War.' Consequently, we are not inclined to think of them as 'The Good Guys'. We are introduced to the character of War when she is cheerfully inducing a massacre at a peace treaty, to Famine when he is revelling in corrupting the world's appetite through a capitalist scheme, to Pollution as they overlook a ruined stream, and to Death as they herald the end of all things with the satisfied words: 'Finally.' When the children eventually face the Horsepeople, we know who we are supposed to support. Yet the account of Revelation tells us otherwise. The four Riders, who bring with them violence and death for people living on earth, are called into the world not by the devil, but by the Lamb of God himself.

This incident of divine punishment is by no means anomalous in the biblical text. God has a history of sending supernatural power to deal out punishment. A flood to destroy a wayward people. An angel of death to wreak vengeance on a gentile power. A rain of burning sulphur upon an immoral city. It may be justified, it may be appropriate or proportionate to the crimes committed and we may believe that God's reasons are 'ineffable,' but these actions are undeniably violent. Unavoidably unpleasant. When I was seven I had a babysitter. Whilst watching The Lion, the Witch and the Wardrobe one evening, we discussed faith. She said she did not believe in God. I asked why. She promptly answered: 'Because God killed all those Egyptians' babies. They were innocent. That wasn't fair. How can he be loving if he does that?' It's a question that gives pause. It did when I was seven, and it still does now. After all, it was Richard Dawkins who said: 'The God of the Old Testament is arguably the most unpleasant character in all fiction; jealous and proud of it; a petty, unjust, unforgiving control-freak; a vindictive, bloodthirsty, ethnic cleanser [...]'[3] and whilst we might disagree with some of his adjectives, the reasoning behind it cannot be faulted. How can a peace-loving God condone violence?

It's an uncomfortable question. Yet, if we are to give the Bible the true respect it deserves, it is a question with which we need to engage. Some might suggest that we follow Aziraphale's lead – accept the divine plan for what it is: 'ineffable'. However, when we do this, when we try and hide the horror of God's violence in piety, we do our own faith a disservice. Greg Boyd, in his interesting work The Crucifixion of the Warrior God, says that when we do this we lose something. 'What is lost is our integrity. What is lost, at least to some degree, is our moral sensitivity to violence.' And should we not be sensitive to violence? After all, the crucifixion is deliberately violent, deliberately horrific, and 'attempting to soften the revolting nature of this offensive material to protect God's character is no different than attempting to soften the revolting nature of the crucifixion to protect God's character.'[4] When we sanitize the darker parts of the bible, when we refuse to engage with the uncomfortable questions, are we disallowing ourselves the opportunity to engage deeply with the divine revelation of scripture?

I agree with Greg Boyd when he says that 'a true respect for the bible involves accepting it as it actually is.' We cannot wish the violence of God away, so let us engage with it. How do you feel about a violent God? Is God's violence fair? What are your ideas about how we can reconcile a peaceful Christ with a vengeful God in the Old Testament?

CREATIVE REFLECTION
A job well done
Since the end of days it had been rather hard to find a comfy place for a spot of dinner. Word had it that there was still a good place on the Isle of Patmos. At least, this was according to Pestilence who always had the best information about gyros. So they had set off from Jerusalem, getting special dispensation from the armies of Heaven to cross through the west bank, and then pretty much sticking to the M5 through Lebanon, Syria and Turkey.

'Shall I check the ferry times?' Famine said, dismounting and sauntering over to the battered timetable in Bodrum harbour.

'Has he forgotten, do you suppose, that time has stopped?' War asked. 'It's been twenty past four for … well, who knows?'

Famine returned.

'What time is it due?'

'Twenty past four.'

War rolled her eyes.

They bribed the ferryman with cigarettes and the four riders stomped onto the deck to sit in the frayed deckchairs, their steeds tied to the railings.

'I wonder if they'll have chicken or beef,' War said.

Pestilence looked over the oil spills as the hull of the ferry cut through them.

'I quite fancy lamb. When in Greece.'

War was the last of them to be in Patmos.

She blinked, frowning up one street, then another.

'Give me a minute, it's been a while. Things looked different in 1945. This way.'

The horsemen fell into single file behind her, the chainmail on her armoured horse clinking in the dead air of the empty street. There was a gurgling sound. They looked at Famine, who in turn looked at his stomach wistfully.

Finally, they saw a glimmer of a warm light in a window. The painted sign for the taverna hung loosely over the doorway.

'Smells good,' War said.

'They make their own souvlaki,' Pestilence said.

'That sounds delicious,' Famine sighed.

A figure appeared in the doorway, a raised rolling pin in hand.

'Fýge! Fýge! Go away! Go away!'

A portly woman with grey hair scraped back in a knot and flour on her apron glared at them all. War stopped advancing.

'We're not with the army,' she said.

'Or the other army!' Pestilence put in.

'We're just here for some gyros.'

The woman shook her head. 'Óchi, I know you – ' she pointed a stubby angry finger at each of them in turn: 'You are the ones who started all this mess!'

'We were only doing our job,' Pestilence said.

She slammed the door. The golden light in the window was extinguished with a puff of infuriated breath.

The horsemen sat in the half dark of the dead sun. Then Death spoke.

'No good deed,' Death said.

GET CREATIVE!

Welcome to the end of Chapter 1! We invite you to explore the show using your own imagination and creativity.

Reflecting

We've explored whether or not God has a plan. What do you think? If you believe God does have a plan but find it hard to have clarity on how that applies to you, we've suggested an activity that you can do during the coming week.

Sometimes it's helpful to write or draw out a representation of your experiences to see if any themes emerge. We've seen this done using the idea of a branching tree, or a river, or a bubble diagram, as well as linear examples like a timeline. Use whatever representation you are most drawn to.

- Can you see patterns or themes you recognise?
- Do you see evidence of a plan, or is there another word that better captures the expression of God's desires for you and your communities?
- In the Christian tradition, God's will is wide and there are many good things out there. What opportunities have you noticed for multiple good choices in the path your life has taken?

Write something
This week, we've seen the International Express Man go to extraordinary lengths to deliver his parcels. Tell us a story about the delivery man. Do you think he demonstrates this level of commitment to all his deliveries? Where is the furthest he has to go for a delivery? Is this the oddest task he's ever been instructed to fulfil? Perhaps you could imagine his job interview!

Make something
The delivery man delivers lots of parcels! (Some have very odd shapes). Can you make a papercraft parcel with a surprise inside? Or perhaps even bake a parcel cake?

If these aren't your thing, that's ok: transformative works take many forms and there are lots of options! Art, knitting, poetry, cartoons, leather working, carpentry, whatever you enjoy. What matters is not quality, but fun.

Don't forget to share your creations with the world! #goodomens @IneffablyLovely on Twitter.

CHAPTER TWO

Body and Matter: Some Body to Love

'The Word became flesh and made his
dwelling among us.'
John 1:14

'It's the solids …. They're trapped…. Confined to a single
shape, a single perspective… it's so limiting.'
Odo (the shape-shifting policeman),
Deep Space Nine

BIBLE READING
Romans 12:1–2

Prayer

It's hard to be bodies.
If we're to follow you and offer our bodies as holy places,
Transform our minds.
Show us the ways our will might not be the thing that
    frees us.
Where our view of our self and our world is distorted,
Help us live embodied and awake.
So we can know what good, pleasing and perfect is,
God-in-us and with-us.
Amen

STARTING ACTIVITY

Reflect on the Bible passage above using the prompt questions below in whatever way you find most beneficial to you. Sketch, scrapbook, scribble in the margins of your Bible, write a song, ponder it while you're in the shower (these last two can be done at the same time), type up some notes.

1. What does it mean to be holy?
2. How do you offer your body as a living sacrifice?
3. What expectations can you identify as 'the pattern of this world' as regards to your body? How might this be different for someone else's body?
4. How might God's 'good, pleasing and perfect will' for a person's body require the transformation of their mind?

TO START YOU THINKING

'Gosh!' says the TV space explorer.* 'This species has evolved so far/advanced their technology/attained enough knowledge/ become so spiritually attuned that they've ascended to a higher plane of existence and become beings of pure energy!'

'You're not a body,' says the pastor. 'You *have* a body. You are a soul.'

We'll let you look up the lyrics to Norman Greenbaum's 1969 song 'Spirit in the Sky' yourself, but the implication is clear enough: if you're holy, you're *above* all that.

The world of *Good Omens* takes its inspiration from a particular version of Western Christian understanding. It goes like this: Heaven and Hell are engaged in a pitched battle to the death for which the world is the battleground. Christians will be okay, though, because this material reality is only a temporary place of suffering, and a chosen (or choosing) few get be whisked off to heaven where everything is perfect, unchanging and spiritual. The rest of you? Take the down escalator.

Your experiences may vary. Can you relate to this? Is this your general understanding of the faith? If not, what's different about the way you see things?

This Christian narrative, in which matter is irrelevant and bodies are disgusting, is one that *Good Omens* riffs on, gleefully subverts and – ultimately – dismisses as a mistake. Crowley's instinct to run away to Alpha Centauri is understandable, but if the story had ended with Aziraphale and Crowley taking to space in the Bentley like Danny and Sandy at the end of *Grease* we'd have been disappointed – even if Adam had decided of his own initiative to save humanity rather than accept his prescribed role as the Destroyer. The 'Great Plan' may revolve around the destruction of Earth and the conflict between Heaven and Hell, but God's Ineffable Plan seems – insofar

(*It doesn't matter which sci-fi TV show, this happens in all of them.)

as the characters can discern – to favour Her embodied creations, their choices, and their care for The World.

For many, many people though, an exclusive Heaven as a disembodied place of safety and superiority *is* Christianity. The idea that bodies are lesser and even dangerous is one that's wormed its way into secular values too, becoming part of 'the pattern of this world.' Fascinatingly, this is reflected in fan-fiction based on the show and there's at least one *Good Omens* fannish trope that trades on this notion ('We can't have a physical relationship! You'll Fall!' 'Don't be silly. It's not a sin if it's love, dear.')

New Testament scholars Tom Wright[1] and Paula Gooder,[2] both drawing on the writings of St Paul, point out that the rejection of the physical is less a Gospel understanding of the universe than it is a Platonic one. Plato described the material world as a degenerate reflection of the real-reality, which is on some other plane of existence where everything is perfect. Wright argues that in this escapist model there's no room for bodily resurrection or 'God's kingdom come on earth, as it is in heaven.' Heaven, Wright insists, is not the Christian's true and final home and the end goal is not discorporation, but 'a new bodily life, after a time of being bodily dead'.

Christian escapism, on the other hand, allows us to abdicate responsibility for material concerns or to withdraw from ourselves and others; if the body is bad and what matters is on the inside, you don't need to look after it. Paula Gooder notes that even body-positive Christians, by minimising the importance of bodies or being silent on what they mean for us, 'can easily suggest that the body is something to be controlled, not loved; ignored and overcome rather than cherished.' (Body, 2016). Authors like Rachel Mann,[3] Nadia Bolz-Weber,[4] Glennon Doyle[5] and Jamie Lee Finch[6] have described experiences of trauma and shame generated by religious and cultural beliefs about the body, as well as pointing towards what a joyful theology of the body might look like. Opinions on what a Christian theology of bodies *should* be differ wildly, even amongst the authors we list above. All agree, though, that it can take many years, along with courage and hard work, to regain a healthy body and mind after being immersed in theologies that emphasise the spiritual over the physical.

Likewise, if the world is irrelevant and all you're interested in is going to some other place when you die, then it doesn't matter what you do to the planet because it isn't your permanent home. The political outworkings of this attitude continue to leave their mark on the Earth – as Adam laments in Episode 5 of the show. Pope Francis, in his Letter *Laudato Si'*[7] warns us that 'Care For Our Common Home' is a matter of life or death to 'the most vulnerable people on the planet,' along with countless non-human species. Christian escapism kills.

We also have Christ's incarnation and resurrection to contend with. If the spiritual is all that matters, Jesus's role is only to be born and to die, opening the cosmic escape hatch for saved souls to depart for heavenly places. But for a while, Jesus as God, as human, had hairy legs, arms, *armpits*, not to mention the logistics that go with being human in an era where they hadn't yet invented toilet paper. A disembodied God can't share meals with their friends, be raised from the dead, ask someone to touch the wound in their side. A God that rejects the physical would likely not invite us to remember them with bread and wine.

As C. S. Lewis points out in *Mere Christianity*,[8] 'There is no good trying to be more spiritual than God. God never meant man to be a purely spiritual creature. That is why He uses material things like bread and wine to put the new life into us. We may think this rather crude and unspiritual. God does not: He invented eating. He likes matter. He invented it.'

Facing as we are the global environmental crisis, increasing social pressures to 'perfect' our bodies, and navigating a cultural legacy of racism, misogyny, homophobia, binary thinking, and Christian escapism, our own theology is worth examining. Perhaps, as in *Good Omens*, a holy connection with our bodies and the world has been God's purpose all along.

FURTHER QUESTIONS

1. Does our theology involve escaping or staying to save the world?
2, Does your experience of your body bring a certain perspective on the world?
3, Living in/as a body is really hard – for some of us more than others. Does the idea of being free of your body after death represent hope for you? Why?
4. What does Christ's incarnation mean to you?
5. What does Jesus experience being born in a human body that a non-embodied being might not?

WATCH: GABRIEL AND BODIES
Gabriel interrupts Aziraphale's sushi dinner (Episode 1, 12:50 – 14:30)

Aziraphale is getting sushi, inhaling in blissful anticipation, when his superior, the Archangel Gabriel, appears to spoil the moment. Gabriel asks Aziraphale why, as an angel – presumably not needing the sustenance – he consumes *that*. Aziraphale's explanations cycle through initial delight in something he seems to think should be self-evident ('It's sushi!') and then a description of the benefit ('It's nice!') and then, resigned and subdued, an excuse ('It's what humans do'). If he's going to pass, Aziraphale has to keep up appearances, of course. Gabriel eschews both food and drink – 'I do not sully the celestial temple of my body with gross matter' – but he does like the clothes. What a shame Armageddon will be along soon to end it all …

PROMPT QUESTIONS

1. How does Aziraphale react to Gabriel's questions about eating and drinking? Why does he feel the need to give several answers?
2. What do you think is Gabriel's relationship with his body?
3. What does the idea of our bodies being 'temples' mean to you? How does it impact your self-image?

GOING DEEPER

Alex reflects:

There's a moment in the 2008 Guillermo Del Toro film Hellboy II: The Golden Army where the hard-living and jovial hero encourages his lovesick best friend to drown his sorrows in cheap beer. 'My body is a temple!' objects the flustered and usually ascetic humanoid amphibian, Abe Sapien. 'It's an amusement park!' growls Hellboy, good-naturedly, before the two go off and get sozzled together.

'I do not sully the celestial temple of my body with gross matter,' says Gabriel, in the clip we watched above, and it's a damning indictment of Aziraphale's simple joy in his meal!

Temples, for me, bring to mind the Parthenon, the Forum in Rome and empty Victorian follies by sculpted lakes. That classical look: all white limestone: unused, unlived in and empty.

Heaven, in the universe of Good Omens – Gabriel's external 'celestial temple', if you will – is a similarly barren, clinical and pristine space. It's bright, and white and full of light. There's no clutter. Nothing personal. No signs of life or something as necessary to living as food, or a body, which Gabriel seems to take to mean as something less than spiritual, not holy. Sully, he says. Gross matter. His disgust is palpable.

We often use this phrase as Gabriel does, to mean we should be careful what we let into our bodies in case we irreparably distort something fragile and easily besmirched. Matter, we're expected to understand, is dirty. Food is particularly dangerous. It's everywhere – advertisements for 'clean eating', images that stoke the fear of putting things inside us and the consequences of consuming too much. Much of it is in the service of selling us things that we can purchase or do to absolve us of our fear of falling short of Gabriel's inhuman pristine ideal. This is what we are supposed to be, a neo-classical temple: clean, sharp, vertical columns of whiteness. Free of wobbles, or melanin, or blemishes, or wrinkles, or disease, or variety in shape. God, or indeed Gabriel, forbid that we age, or we are born – or stray – outside what society wishes us to be, or that our bodies change through circumstances or our own choices. As Gabriel points out, 'It's so ... human.' We wear the proof of our imperfect humanity in our bodies, and we, like Aziraphale, are often shamed.

This use of the metaphor of the body as a temple is not a godly one. Not in the show, where God's purposes are very different from those of Heaven's. And not in the Bible, where the metaphor means something very different. Our notions of purity have little to do with Jesus.

True, purity was an important concept Jesus' time, although it's doubtful it has the meaning we imbue it with today. For starters – in the days when 'washed in the blood of the lamb' wasn't just a metaphor beloved of Christian Union songbooks – Gabriel's celestial temple would look more like a butcher's shop.

The temple that the apostle Paul, from whom we get the phrase (1 Corinthians 6:19), and Jesus (John 2:19, Mark 14:58) refer to, is the place where *God is present* in this world made of matter.[9] For Jews, the inner room of the Temple was the one place where God's presence physically existed on earth. For Paul, post-Pentecost, it is *our bodies* that are the place where the Holy Spirit makes Her home. Our bodies are temples because, here on earth, they are *the place God is*.

In this model there's little point in a celestial (i.e. heavenly) temple because, as noted for example in the vision recorded in Revelation 21:22, God's presence is everywhere.

Despite the popular vernacular, Christian beliefs and practices centre bodies as the mucky vehicle through which we experience God. There is to be a bodily resurrection; a restoration of the earth; Jesus was born as human, with a body, God incarnate – God embodied; and most Christian traditions adopt a meal as the central practice of worship.

You, as your body, are holy not because you have never been touched by corruption, or – despite the Old Testament purity laws! – stretched by pregnancy, or because your body doesn't work the way you wished, or doesn't measure up to the expectations you and others have for it. Your body is holy because it is where God is.

Jesus seemed to go out of his way to subvert the more exclusionary purity rules anyway: touching lepers, eating, drinking, and generally crossing boundaries that existed to diminish and shame people for being simply people (Matthew 11:19). Gabriel is – as becomes apparent during the course of the show – entirely wrong about the desires of God as pertains to bodies and food.

As Jesus himself points out, 'What goes into someone's mouth does not defile them, but what comes out of their mouth, that is what defiles them' (Matthew 15:11). He goes on to explain to Peter: 'Don't you see that whatever enters the mouth goes into the stomach and then out of the body? But the things that come out of a person's mouth come from the heart, and these defile them.' (Matthew 16:17–18)

Eat that, Gabriel.

FOLLOW UP QUESTIONS

1. Can you describe your own relationship with your body in one word?
2. If you're not from a culture where 'temple' makes you think of ancient Greek and Roman ruins, what images, feelings and thoughts did Gabriel's metaphor bring to

mind? Did you relate to anything in Alex's reflection above? If not, what else did it bring up for you? If you want to share your thoughts, tweet us!

3. If common use of 'Your body is a temple' isn't based on its original context, what other common phrases or even bible verses might you have internalised without context? What difference would that make to how you think about God, other people, yourself or the world? Here's some starting examples:

- Turn the other cheek (Matthew 5:39)
- Go the extra mile (Matthew 5:41)
- An eye for an eye (Exodus 21:24)

WATCH: THE NAMING OF THE HELL-HOUND
Adam names Dog (Episode 1, 45:12 – 48.12)

The Antichrist is supposed to receive a hell-hound on his eleventh birthday. Adam is in the woods, explaining to his friends that he wants a dog. The hell-hound approaches, unseen. It's as big as a horse, drooling, growling, its eyes glow red, its teeth are yellow and bared in a snarl. God narrates the events as they unfold, stressing the importance of the naming moment: As soon as Adam names the hell-hound, Armageddon will begin. The naming gives it 'purpose', 'function', and 'identity'. Adam's describing the kind of dog he wants and the hell-hound is listening. Adam doesn't want a big dog, he wants one who can go down rabbit holes, who's intelligent and can learn tricks. He's going to call it – him – 'Dog'. There's a pop, and the hell-hound assumes his final form. Dog is little with floppy triangular ears and a waggy tail, he yaps as he runs into Adam's arms and whines as Adam scratches behind his ears.

PROMPT QUESTIONS
1. How does Adam impact dog's embodiment?
2. How does our embodiment affect who we are?

GOING DEEPER
Emma reflects:

A tiger pads slowly through the forest, its amber eyes fixated and deadly. A robin hops towards the bird feeder, its feathers ruffled against the breeze and it's head cocked to the noise of the traffic. A small Jack Russell terrier barks merrily and gallops towards his boy owner in the woods, sniffing the air for scents of rabbit holes. There is something pure and joyous about the way other animals inhabit their bodies. There is no questioning of self or purpose, only the rawest instincts of body and mind. To run, to fly, to hunt, to bark – to chase cats and postmen and rabbits down their holes.

I often wonder what it would be like if we humans had kept some of our devolved animal consciousness. I imagine a universe in which our evolution gave us all the fruits God had planned: bipedalism, higher cognitive function and self-awareness, but only a tiny measure of it. What if there were a way we could exist in the universe as we are, but still maintain that animalistic attitude to our bodies? That they are the sacks of meat we live in and run in and sleep in and grow in, but they are not any measure of our value. What if we had no sense of a body that is better than any other, but only that it was the embodiment of the individual? For Dog does not mourn his hell-hound form. Why should he? For he is Dog now, and this is the body of Dog.

I have had an eating disorder for twenty years. It began when I was ten years old, the year of the millennium. When I share this information with people, they want to know how it happened. 'What do you think was the reason?' they often ask. For I was loved, tremendously, by a wonderful family. I was a white, middle-class child growing up in the rural south of England in educational and social privilege. People want to know how such a lucky, lucky girl came to hate her body. I often tell them the likely psychiatric explanation – that it was the earliest manifestation of a mental illness that I now know to be Obsessive Compulsive Disorder – but the truth is that the answer is much more complicated, because so is the question. If the question is not 'Why did you stop eating?' but rather 'Why were you unable to embody yourself with contentment?' then my answer may change. Oh, all the things that answer could be.

It could be that in the year 2000, 16 and 17-year-old girls were still being hired to pose naked on page 3 of The Sun, and the paper would often do 'countdowns' until their legal age. It could be because 'Baby One More Time', the famous music video in which Britney Spears dressed as a sexy school girl was the biggest song of 1999 and boys at school would sing it at us in the corridors, or builders would shout it at you when you walked past in your uniform. It could be that one of the first things I learned in secondary school was which bus drivers were safe and which ones were pervy. It could be that the third wave feminism that embraced Pamela Anderson and Jordan as icons of sexual liberation put pressure on 'good' girls like me to focus on their brains rather than their bodies, while still trying to be pretty enough to be validated. You could call it the Carol Vorderman golden ratio. It could be because Charlie Dimmock was digging gardens with her nipples out, and rather than being celebrated as her choice her nipples became the public property of the nation to leer on. It could be that learning how to live in a woman's body is profoundly conflicting and dangerous.

It could be that, or it could be The Matrix. Or René Descartes. Or Paul the apostle. What do they have in common? They all suggest the idea that our bodies are merely vessels for our consciousness; flawed and broken vessels that ultimately have nothing to do with our true selves. Whilst these concepts have merit (cue a line of well-meaning people saying, 'Don't worry, it's what's on the inside that counts'), they also create problems.

I do not disagree with Paul when he tells us that we will gain new forms after death, forms that suit the holy remaking of the world, I do disagree with a chain of thought that then suggests the forms we inhabit here are unholy. For what comfort is it to a child who faces the institutionalized male gaze scouring every inch of her prepubescent body to say, 'It's all right if your body isn't up to standard – you'll get a new one in heaven?' How does it change and mar her soul to believe she must hate the flesh she is imprisoned in until the Kingdom Comes? If, as Christians, we do value the soul more than the body, then perhaps we should have a stronger consideration of what dismissing the body will do to the soul. Many people have said to me, 'Yes, I understand, it's all right to acknowledge it, but we don't want to become body obsessed! Then we're just like the world!' My answer to that is very simple: the world teaches that nobody is perfect. Surely Christians, who believe in the divine creation, should teach that everybody is.

For what might we be if, rather than carrying our bodies like burdens that are too fat, too old, too big, too black, too brown, too broken, too disabled to be perfect, we inhabited them with the confidence that when the world looked at them, they saw only one thing? Us. The perfect flawless embodiment of a soul.

CREATIVE REFLECTION
Daily Desecration

> Her body is a map;
> The path carved in white and
> Red lines where her skin has
> Stretched and bled.

He has grown and shrunk,
Carried a bloated belly
Or worn his ribs proudly –
White edged medals made of bone.

Their insides are twisted, breath is
fetid from years of acid burning its way
back up to their smile, which is radiant.

They are miracles of flesh,
Alive, still alive.
Not lillies in the field nor weeds,
but still growing in the broken ground.
Following His Voice.

Emma Hinds, 2019

ACTIVITIES

Creative and prophetic counter-cultural activity

Gabriel's notion of 'temple' as divorced from matter isn't a Christian concept. Pick a small (or not-so-small!) thing to do, to rebel against any insidious voices you have that undermine your embodied identity as the place where God makes Their home. Do whatever that looks like for you, if you feel able to do so. Have sushi! Paint those nails! Make a cup of tea! Have sex! Wear your favourite hat. Finally get that tattoo ... Let your bodies show that you lived and do not be ashamed!

Words and embodiment

What words have shaped you? Are there any of these words that God might contradict? What harmful words may have been said about you that you might replace with ones that God prefers? Once you have a list, try writing them on sticky notes and putting them somewhere visible like a mirror!

Make something

We experience the world through our senses. Can you pick a sense and do something to celebrate it? Maybe bake a cake and share it, knit a scarf, put up some shelves, arrange some flowers, listen to music, write a song?

CHAPTER THREE

Power: I Gave it Away!

'Very truly I tell you, unless a kernel of wheat falls to the ground and dies, it remains only a single seed. But if it dies, it produces many seeds.'
John 12:24

'...you could be free. Provided you realized it was one of your options.'
Terry Pratchett, Interesting Times

BIBLE READING
Philippians 2:1 – 11

Prayer
Holy spirit, inspire us.
Grant us the generosity to gift what power we have,
and the courage to assert our humanity when we
  are powerless.
Keep us safe.
Where oppression has become normal, reveal your vision
  for your kingdom.
Give us the imagination to envisage a fairer world, and
  the compassion to desire it.
Show us when we wield our power unawares, and grant
  us the humility to recognise when we need to let go
  and get out of the way so others can thrive.
Amen.

STARTING ACTIVITY
Reflect on the Bible passage above using the prompts below.

1. What power do you have? You could think about your
   workplace, home-life, travel, shopping, hobbies, money,
   culture, race, religion, relationships, inner life, etc.
2. How does 'having the same mind-set as Christ Jesus'
   affect how you exercise that power?

TO START YOU THINKING
'I *gave it away!*' wails Aziraphale, when Crowley asks after the
angel's flaming sword. Crowley is amazed! Relinquishing

God-given power for the sake of those who have none; whoever heard of such a thing?!

Aziraphale prioritises Adam and Eve's needs over his own ambition. In our reading Paul urges us to do likewise (Philippians 2: 3–4). As individuals, as communities, in our wider culture – even, perhaps, between nations – we are to have the same mindset as Christ Jesus, who didn't consider power something to cling to (Phil 2:7), and who said, 'Anyone who wants to be first must be the very last, and the servant of all.' (Mark 9:35).

Philippians 2: 6 – 11 places Jesus in several contexts:

- Jesus before creation, 'being in very nature God'.
- Jesus being born as a baby.
- Jesus as a child, as a refugee.
- Jesus as a grown man, as a Jew in an occupied territory, as a teacher and Rabbi.
- Jesus before Pilate being sentenced to death.
- Jesus on the cross.
- Jesus, exalted to the highest place, with the greatest power and authority.

Thinking about the above, what power does Jesus have in each situation? To what extent is he aware of his power? How does he exert it?

Power, privilege and authority depend on context. Crowley and Aziraphale, for example, have tremendous power by human standards but little, if any, within their respective organisations. Becoming more aware of the balance of power in our culture and relationships helps us avoid putting unnecessary burdens on other people. Working out how to imitate Jesus in practice leads us to ask: who has the power?

To help us think about this, we've made the matrix below.

UNKNOWN POWER	KNOWN POWER
I DON'T REALISE I HAVE POWER, OR THAT I HAVE MORE POWER THAN OTHERS.	I KNOW I HAVE POWER OR AM IN A POSITION OF POWER.
I CAN'T RECOGNISE THAT OTHERS MIGHT NOT HAVE THE SAME ADVANTAGES I DO. OR:	I CAN IDENTIFY THE EXTENTS OF THAT POWER.
I DON'T REALISE I HAVE ANY POWER TO MAKE A DIFFERENCE.	

INCREASING POWER

DECREASING AWARENESS ← → INCREASING AWARENESS

UNKNOWN LACK OF POWER	KNOWN LACK OF POWER
I DON'T HAVE THE CONTEXT TO REALISE I DON'T HAVE POWER, OR THAT I HAVE LESS POWER THAN OTHERS.	I KNOW THAT IN THIS SITUATION I, OR OTHERS, DO NOT HAVE POWER.
I CAN'T IMAGINE THE WORLD BEING DIFFERENT, OR THAT THERE COULD BE A NEED FOR THE WORLD TO BE DIFFERENT.	I CAN IDENTIFY THE EXTENTS TO WHICH I OR OTHERS LACK POWER.

DECREASING POWER

When we know we have power...

Jesus is aware of his power, but rather than use it for his own ambition or even for the good of others, he gave it up. This is challenging for Christians, particularly when we're encouraged to seek political and cultural clout so it can be exercised 'For the Good of the Kingdom' (or for 'God's Fame' or to 'Make Christianity Great Again'). That doesn't seem to be what Jesus models in the gospels.

We see Christ's subversive authority, manifested by his willing sacrifice of power, paralleled in *Good Omens*. Adam Young's original intentions are good – he wants things to be better – but his power over all the kingdoms of the world comes at the cost of submitting to Hell. When invited to rule with the Devil, Adam – like Jesus (Matthew 4:8–10) –

ultimately rejects this temptation. Rather than taking control to remake the world on his own terms, he surrenders his power, submits to his father's authority, and becomes like a little child. He forfeits his role as the antichrist with actions that are decidedly Christ-like.

Enacting this in our own lives, though, assumes we have power to give away. If we're already at the mercy of others, following the advice in Philippians 2 can leave our relationships or cultural dynamics open to abuse.

When we know we don't have power...
Have you ever met anyone who can't stop giving time, energy, or money such that they burn out or neglect themselves or their families? Perhaps you've ended up comforting a person who hurt you and prioritising their wellbeing over yours. Church can become a place where giving unconditionally is encouraged, but without reciprocity that can lead to guilt, bitterness and resentment. Trying to give power away when you don't have it can also lead to putting yourself in dangerous situations.

Is this what Paul means when he asks us to consider others' interests before our own? Perhaps there are other verses we can look to for wisdom in this context. 'I am sending you out like sheep among wolves,' says Jesus, to his disciples, 'Therefore be as shrewd as snakes and as innocent as doves.' (Matthew 10:16). He also warns us against willingly taking the role of doormat (Matthew 7:6). We can be faithful and still exercise our power to draw boundaries and learn to say 'no'. When someone is your enemy and you can't choose to leave the situation, Jesus advocates going the extra mile, turning the other cheek, giving someone the last of your clothes (Matthew 5:38–42) – all of which are actions that draw attention to the power others have over you, and confront those people with your humanity and vulnerability. This gives your enemies the option to choose to consider you; it gives them the opportunity to change without putting yourself in further danger. Unfortunately, this doesn't guarantee a good outcome. That relies on them being compassionate and self-aware enough to notice.

When we're unaware of our own power
It's prophetic work to identify unnoticed power so we can challenge and encourage ourselves and each other.

Not realising our power or its effects can lead to hurting people. We see this when the prophet Nathan rebukes King David (2 Samuel 12:1–14). David is unaware of (or unwilling to acknowledge) the unjust way he's wielded his power. It takes Nathan telling the story from a different angle to make David realise the consequences of his actions. Sometimes it's necessary to listen to those who point out how our power hurts others, and it can be painful to acknowledge that. There's an unattributed phrase that goes, 'To those accustomed to privilege, equality feels like oppression.' And it does! Humble pie is the worst! Loss of power can feel like dying, but the process comes with a promise. Jesus uses the metaphor of seeds (John 12:24), and tells us that in relinquishing our life we find something greater.

Alternatively, if you don't realise you have the power to change things you may have a beautiful gift you never even considered! This is where prophetic encouragement comes in. The children facing the Four Horsemen at Tadfield Airbase don't think they've got power: these are *grown ups*! Can't Adam see that? Adam knows three of the Horsemen have only the power we allow them to have: they aren't real, they are 'humanity's nightmares' – the product of human choices. The children have options, Adam assures them: 'just say what you believe'.

If all you've known is war, peace may not seem possible, but Pepper has vision. She quotes two powerful prophets: her mother, who gifted her with perspective ('my mum says war is just masculine imperialism!'), and Tori Amos, the singer who believes in peace. Pepper dispatches War with a prophetic act, by declaring the possibility of peace.

Change is hard and awkward work, but the first step is being able to imagine something different. Sometimes that can come from prophets or friends bringing insight to bear on unjust situations. We can also seek out the perspectives of people who are hurting, or use our imaginations and listen to the voice from within.

When our disadvantage and lack of power is invisible to us

Witchfinder-Sergeant Shadwell is a hilarious example of someone oblivious to his powerlessness. He's convinced his finger can make people disappear, and he's utterly mistaken! We're going to explore how absence or imbalance of power can go unnoticed when we talk about Agnes later in this chapter.

PROMPT QUESTIONS

1. How should Christians measure value?
2. What does that mean for the kinds of power we value?
3. What kinds of power do you find the hardest to give away?

WATCH: AGNES NUTTER, WITCH
Agnes is arrested and burned at the stake (Episode 2, 8:00 – 12:25).

Lancashire, 1656, the last witch-burning in England. Newt's forebear Witchfinder Major Thou-Shalt-Not-Commit-Adultery Pulsifer leads an angry mob to arrest Anathema's ancestor, Agnes Nutter. She is to be burned at the stake. The villagers all agree she must die: her crimes include advocating a healthy lifestyle, curing her neighbours' illnesses, accidentally discovering acupuncture, and prophesying the future (with never-failing accuracy, as it happens). Agnes has pre-empted her sentence and built her own pyre – 'Very irregular, Mistress Nutter,' – which brings an explosive end to her life and a fatal revenge on her executioners.

PROMPT QUESTIONS

1. How are power and weakness represented in this scene?
2. Agnes seems to have several presumably-God-given powers. How does she choose to use them?
3. How do the villagers react to the way Agnes exercises her power? Why?
4. Jesus, in the Sermon on the Mount, declares that we will know true prophets by their fruit (Matthew 7:15–23). What is the fruit of Agnes's life's work?

GOING DEEPER

Five hundred years before the fictional Agnes Nutter, Hildegard von Bingen (1098 – 1179) was writing her own books of prophecy. She was a medieval genius: a composer, naturalist, theologian, teacher, administrator, public speaker and writer who advised fellow church leaders for miles around, corresponded with emperors and popes, toured Europe in her late sixties, and invented her own language. Her books explore the structure of the universe, natural histories of plants and animals, medical remedies and the practicalities of sex and reproduction, as well as recording her mystical visions and divine ecstasy.[1]

Jesus talks in Matthew 7:15–23 about how we discern whether others are acting in accordance with God's will. Are they real prophets, or do they look outwardly good but are at their core destructive? 'You will know them by their fruits,' says Jesus. In other words, what are the consequences of their words and actions? We can turn this question on ourselves; verses 21 to 23 warn against self-deception and indicate that it's actions, not labels, that make the ultimate difference in whether or not we're aligning ourselves with Jesus.

It can be difficult to tell what is and isn't the right or good thing to do. Where do we stand on the moral issues of our lives and the important cultural questions of the day? Often, the right thing depends on the context, as Paul explores in Chapter 14 of his letter to the Romans, and – as Jesus points out in Matthew 7:1–5 – we're not always best placed to make that call.

Morals can look different in retrospect. Hildegard of Bingen's works of music, art and literature are still appreciated today. She accomplished extraordinary things for a woman of her time and she has been celebrated by modern feminists. But the idea that women have equal worth to men is a much later philosophy; Hildegard herself emphasised her 'womanish weakness' and frequently used 'womanish' as a term of criticism.[2]

Hildegard saw the world and herself through the lenses of her culture's power dynamics, which favoured men. This imbalance of power dictated – and continues to dictate – how people spoke, what they valued, what they expected from life. In Hildegard's case, passivity, submission and receiving were seen as what women were suited for, and whether she internalised this because it was the only view her culture allowed her, or whether it was the only way she could be confident in finding an audience, Hildegard portrayed herself as a simple vessel for her visions.

Not only was Hildegard unable to challenge the patriarchal assumptions of the time, the unusual nature of her call actually supported the medieval understanding of the natural order of things. Men in the church argued that since God uses what is weak and foolish to shame the wise and strong (1 Corinthians 1:27), it was entirely in His character to use a woman as the instrument of His revelations – it affirmed her subordinate status! What we now understand to be a cultural balance of power was interpreted as God-ordained. Hildegard, a woman of undeniable strength, was still an anomaly for women of her era. It would be another few hundred years before the inferior status of women would be seriously challenged in Europe.

In the scene we watched earlier, Agnes – another woman of undeniable strength – suffers the consequences of exerting that strength. It's not clear why her work is so offensive to her neighbours, but we can guess. Are they concerned that the source of her power is demonic? Are they offended by a woman shamelessly wielding unusual power? Are they frightened by things they don't understand? For these or other reasons, the verdict is plain; although everything the villagers share with the witchfinder is an action that has good fruit, obviously Agnes needs to be destroyed.

Agnes couldn't serve her community without bringing down the wrath of the authorities on herself. She dies for it: choosing to accept her fate but also – in a decidedly un-Jesus-like manoeuvre! – dealing out bloody revenge. Hildegard, in the real world, worked within her culture's limitations. Both Agnes and Hildegard are navigating what we now call a structural injustice: the harm caused by inherited social structures (politics, economy, culture, prejudice, military or para-military control) that mean some groups find it much easier to have a voice, choices, and control over their lives and the lives of others.

On a personal level, it can be hard to decide whether to challenge unjust power structures; to work within them as a prophetic voice for change (neither of which Agnes or Hildegard did directly); or to leave them – where that's possible – to find a fairer environment in which to thrive (an option not open to our heroines here!). All of these options can be 'right' in different circumstances.

According to Matthew 7, we need to keep our eyes open to discern whether or not we're working alongside Jesus. Interrogating the outcomes of our words and actions, and listening with humility to the experiences of others, is therefore important. Perhaps, in a world where there are many battles still to be fought against prejudice, listening to those who are different from us is a good place to start.

FOLLOW UP QUESTIONS

1. What do you think constitutes 'good fruit'?
2. When do you find it difficult to know whether you're doing the right thing or not? How do you decide?
3. How do you interpret Jesus' words in Matthew 7:21 – 23, which seem to imply that there's no particular religious label required for a person or community to 'know' Jesus? Would taking this statement at face value require you to relinquish any kind of power? How would that feel? What would that look like?
4. It's easy for structural injustices, which within a culture often masquerade as common sense, to fall into the 'unknown lack' quadrant of our power matrix at the start of the chapter. Can you give an example from your own life or the life of someone close to you, when you or they have faced prejudice or structural injustice? How do you or they navigate that?
5. We've discussed the role of women in society, but can you think of other cultural assumptions that are frequently spoken of as being the natural or God-ordained order? How might these change in the future?

WATCH: CROWLEY AT THE CROSS
The crucifixion of Jesus (Episode 3, 2:48 – 4:30)

As Roman soldiers nail Jesus to a wooden frame, Jesus begs: 'Father, please, you have to forgive them. They don't know what they are doing!' People look on, grief-stricken. So do two immortal beings. Gender and shape are optional to angels and demons: Crowley's red curls flutter in the breeze as they escape her headdress. Her expression is grim. Aziraphale stands next to her, flinching as the metal stakes are hammered in. They talk: Crowley's had a name change and, it appears, was the tempter who met Jesus in the desert. Crowley asks what Jesus said to get himself crucified; Aziraphale informs her that it was 'Be kind to each other.' Crowley isn't surprised that such a message would lead to a death sentence. They stand watch until the skies, and the camera, fade to black.

PROMPT QUESTIONS

1. Neil Gaiman has said that Crowley is presenting as female in this scene,[3] as well as the scenes in which she's employed as Warlock's nanny. Given the importance of women in the crucifixion and resurrection stories, what do you make of the demon presenting as a woman and the angel not?

2. The Bible uses female descriptors and metaphors for God in many places (for example: Job 38:29, Proverbs 1:20–21, Isaiah 66:13, Luke 13:31–35 and Matthew 23:37–39) and many Christians venerate Mary, the mother of Jesus. Does reflecting on these passages, and – if you can – considering using different pronouns for God, change how you perceive God in your mind? Does it change how you feel?

3. What do you make of Aziraphale's summary of Jesus' message? What does it mean to be kind? How might kindness (as opposed to 'niceness') relate to our theme of power?

GOING DEEPER

There's a world-building tidbit in Episode 6 that's interesting in light of the show's portrayal of the crucifixion.

While giving a pep-talk, Dagon ('Lord of the Files') reminds us that the demons of the show are veterans of a 'Glorious Revolution' that they, the rebels, lost. We're left to assume that these demons were originally angels; that their Fall transformed their nature in ways that are apparently physical and probably psychological; that there's an occult/ ethereal hierarchy, and demons are at the bottom. They were cast out of Heaven not (or not only) because they're literally revolting, but because they fought, lost and were banished.

Crowley is, as far as we know, a demon of no importance and therefore a relatively junior member of an exiled group who have been humiliated and forced to work in unsavoury conditions. He's not a Duke of Hell or a Prince. He's just a grunt, and one that mostly works a long way away from Head Office surrounded by very different daily influences. His colleagues are pretty awful: they frighten him and don't seem to respect him. His good (bad?) standing with Hell is only worth the success of his latest Temptation, and his life is precarious, being as it is at the whim of his boss: a terrifying and powerful being who can contact him anywhere. Crowley is intruded upon in his home, in his beloved car, in a deserted cinema. He has no refuge that offers guaranteed safety or privacy. Like many a human woman in this situation (Tamar in Genesis 38:1–26, Naomi in Ruth 3:1–15, much of history), he has to resort to trickery and manipulation if he wants to exert power amongst his peers. Crowley is a being who exists on the margins even within the marginalised group he's part of. On Earth, unlike Aziraphale, his snake-like eyes mean he doesn't pass for human either. He doesn't fit in Heaven, Earth or Hell.

It's interesting, then, when it's established on-screen that Crowley and Jesus – a man well known for hanging out with society's rejects – were acquainted.

In Luke 10:25 – 37, Jesus is posed a question: 'Who is my neighbour?' Jesus' answer is the Parable of the Good Samaritan. The neighbour, says Jesus, is the one who had mercy on the victim of violence who lay powerless at the side of the road.

In Good Omens, as with the priest and the Levite, the

beings whose roles and job titles mean we expect them to do the saving don't actually care, and our heroes are those who choose to act out of compassion despite having good reasons not to. In this at least, *Good Omens* aligns its narrative message with the teaching of Jesus. Both *Good Omens* and the Parable of the Good Samaritan subvert our expectations of characters based on their positions, suggesting that it's not inherent nature that defines our goodness, but our actions (see also Matthew 7:20). When priests and authorities (or angels) are focussed on maintaining their purity, boundaries and moral superiority, they are the ones we want to avoid becoming, and an Enemy (Samaritan or demon) who defies expectations and rejects cultural taboos to act kindly is the one we should emulate.

Crowley seems to grasp this instinctively. His angelic counterpart does not, even when faced with evidence to the contrary and an obvious desire to believe otherwise. Aziraphale insists that there are beings that are inherently good and others that are inherently evil throughout most of the show, resulting in a heart-wrenching break-up scene in Episode 3.

It's clear that we're meant to root for Crowley as he reaches across boundaries towards Aziraphale, when he asks questions founded in compassion, when he argues that humanity, like the man left by the side of the road, is worth saving. It's said explicitly in the very beginning: 'Funny thing, if I did the right thing and you did the wrong one.' Funny or not, Crowley has the right of it and it's Aziraphale that can't see the joke. It takes 6000 years for Aziraphale to let go of his jingoistic tendencies.

It's therefore not a massive surprise, it is in fact really rather touching, that Crowley's presenting as female at the crucifixion. Crowley has always been the one who's outside of the powerful structures, who is forced into a prescribed role then (as with Tamar in Genesis 38:24, Naomi in

Ruth 1:19–20 and – again – much of history) mocked and rejected when he exercises his agency through the only options available. Crowley knows you can't trust the institution to have your best interests at heart. Crowley, as with many women in the gospels, is at the moral heart of the story. He tries to tell the truth and galvanise others to action and isn't believed. Of course, Crowley's a woman watching Jesus.

FOLLOW UP QUESTIONS

1. If you feel like we're being too down on Aziraphale, don't worry, we'll get to him later. Why do you think he finds it hard to let go of the notion that some groups are inherently good, whereas some are inherently not?
2. Aziraphale describes angels and demons as 'hereditary enemies', but if so, who did they inherit their enmity from? Whose interests does that rivalry – in which there are two sides and no wiggle room – serve?
3. Are there any enmities or dislikes you've inherited? If there are, can you identify a power imbalance in that enmity? What does that mean for how you think about it or navigate it?

CREATIVE REFLECTION
His Options For Travel Are Limited

The man from Galilee dines amongst friends, sharing bread and terrible jokes. Against his chest the youngest, John, reclines. He is eating a fig.

'Tell me a story,' demands John. Jesus sucks his teeth, thinking.

'Did I tell you of the Accuser in the wilderness?' he asks.

'No,' says John, mouth full. 'Was he ugly? Were you scared?'

'I think he was a she,' says Jesus.

'A woman!' asks John, with, craning his neck to look up with interest. 'Did she tempt you?'

Across the room, one of the Marys rolls her eyes. Jesus flicks John in the ear.

Not like that,' he tuts. 'She asked: *If you're the Son of God, why don't you turn these stones to bread? Feed the hungry, save the starving, that sort of thing?*'

'And you said no?'

'Man cannot live on bread alone, John.'

John picks at the remaining half of his fig. 'And then?' he asks.

'She showed me how little children suffer in every kingdom of the world and said: *We could rescue all of them. Pledge allegiance to Hell, and you can take charge.* I told her we must worship God alone.'

'Then what?' asks young John.

'She tried to get me to jump from the top of the temple,' Jesus tells him.

John frowns. 'Why?' he asks, through a mouth full of fruit.

'I think she thought it would be funny,' says Jesus.

'Huh,' says John, and swallows.

Jesus pokes him in the shoulder. 'Are you going to write this down?' he asks.

'Nah,' says John, pinching another fig and getting comfy.

Behind them, hunched over a wax tablet, Matthew scribbles furiously.

Alex Booer, 2019

GET CREATIVE!
Writing prompt!

Episode 3 shows Crowley and Aziraphale bearing witness to a tiny handful of moments from history. Do you have any favourite periods in history or Bible stories where you can imagine these two beings meeting up? Perhaps they're possessing famous people at key historical moments? Did Crowley start the Great Fire of London? How did Aziraphale cope with Rationing? If you're so inclined, you could make art, write a short story or poem.

Imagine a future ...
Interrogating what passes for common sense can reveal the sicknesses underlying our cultural assumptions. What frustrations are you living with that you've accepted as normal? What can you change? What can't you change? Imagine a world where it could be different. Ask for insight from God, who can do immeasurably more than you can ask or imagine (Ephesians 3:20). If you like, write, draw or record your desires.

And relax ...
If you're labouring under the daily realities of structural injustice, it can be therapeutic to imagine a world where these stressors are absent. This is one of the reasons fan-fiction and speculative fiction can be so attractive for groups with relatively little cultural power. There are so many fan-fiction stories written by women which star strong, male characters who invest in therapy, take responsibility for their mental health and commit to growing their emotional intelligence! Stories can also be a way for people to explore characterisations which might be side-lined in the mainstream media, for example with regard to race, gender, religion or sexuality. There are some great Jewish *Good Omens* fan-stories!

CHAPTER FOUR
Beliefs: We Believe

'Religious and philosophical beliefs are, indeed, as
dangerous as fire, and nothing can take from them
that beauty of danger.'
G. K. Chesterton, 'Heretics'

'You believe that there is one God. Good! Even the
demons believe that – and shudder.'
James 2:19

BIBLE READING
Ephesians 1:3–14

STARTING ACTIVITY

1. Think about the passage above. Paul uses words like *predestined, chosen, will* and *purpose* to describe the idea that specific things are planned by God in advance. To what extent do you think that applies to your own life and communities?

2. Consider the rest of the words in this passage. For example, in verses 4 to 8 we have: *blessing, holy, blameless, love, adoption, sonship, pleasure, grace, redemption, forgiveness, riches, lavished*. What does this suggest about the divine plan Paul is talking about? Does thinking about these words influence how you feel about this reading, or the idea of God having a plan?

Prayer

Your will is Grace, Love, Pleasure:
Kindness like honey
Endless joy.

Help us to listen.
So as we choose how we Act Justly, Love Mercy and walk humbly,
We can accept the grace, love and pleasure offered to us
In the sweetness of your presence.

That we might know we are loved, and our neighbours are indeed loved.

TO START YOU THINKING

Consider Anathema. She and her ancestors devote their lives to discerning the meaning of Agnes's prophecies so they can obey them. She wants to do the right thing. As she tells Newt, it causes her anguish when she feels like she's failed and got it wrong.

Does the fact that Anathema tries to follow Agnes' prophesies to the letter mean that she never makes choices? Does Anathema have free will? Do we? What do you think the effect of following Agnes' prophecies has on Anathema's life, her health, her peace of mind and her sense of worth?

They're interesting questions, and they have an impact on the lives of those who wrestle with them, but for good or ill, we're not going to solve the question of predestination and determinism in a short devotional chapter! We'll leave all that to your thoughts and discussions! We're going to focus instead on another question posed by this passage in Paul's letter to the Ephesians: What does being chosen – or, if your tastes run that way, not chosen – mean for you?

As a young graduate engineer, Alex's technical reports were generally pretty good at identifying facts: the site history, the type of soil and rock, the depth to the groundwater table and so forth. Those reports would always be handed back from senior colleagues covered in red pen, concluding with an ellipsis and the words '...*so what?*' Her clients wanted to know how to build a foundation, construct a railway embankment, or fix a landslide. How did the facts she was so pleased to share mean they should actually proceed?

Ephesians 1:4–10 is a narrative arc of the universe, a statement of beliefs about the way the world is. It tells the story of existence from 'before the creation of the world,' to a future 'when the times reach their fulfilment.' But ... so what? What do we construct from this information?

While Paul suggests God has everything planned to the last footnote, these verses don't tell us what that means in practice. There are hints. We are chosen, says Paul, so that, 'We might be for the praise of his glory,' and God's purpose is to 'bring unity to all things,' but that's not exactly specific. Historically, fights were had over the meaning of these verses and people were killed over these arguments, which – if the goal is God's 'good pleasure' – seems to defeat the, well, the *purpose*.

How we frame our existence is important, but scripture warns us against stopping there. 'Faith by itself, if it is not accompanied by action, is dead,' says the writer of the book of James (James 2:17). 'You see that a person is considered righteous by what they do and not by faith alone.' (James 2:24). For James, as for Paul in Philippians 2 and for Jesus throughout the gospels, what we believe and trust in seems to be secondary to how we treat people (Matthew 25:40), and how we order our inner lives (Matthew 5:28).

There's a strong culture in certain strains of Christianity which emphasises accepting the truth of definitive statements – a belief in facts, or doctrine – as the most important thing. But churches that have the same creed or statement of beliefs may interpret God's purposes in very different ways:

- One might welcome divorcees in ministry, whilst another might not.
- One might worship in silence, another with ritual and props, another might be loud and exuberant, another may embrace a range of styles.
- One might have people of all genders in positions of teaching, another may allow only men to preach.
- One might encourage holy mischief and political activism; one might teach that authorities are God-ordained and their directions to be respected.
- One might celebrate and encourage healthy romantic relationships across a spectrum of genders, one may believe marriage is between one man and one woman.

Some of the above are just preference, and some aren't a case of 'either/or' but 'both/and' in healthy balance. Some are exclusive and contradictory moral distinctions. Which are considered righteous? We have to decide what deeds breathe life into our statements of faith. What's right? What's wrong? What actions are good, and which bad? How do we tell? This passage in Ephesians 1 doesn't say. Whether or not we have free will, whether God predestines our fate, we still have to choose how we act.

In this chapter, we look at Aziraphale, as he navigates the realisation that the angels he's worked with for millennia share the same understanding of the universe but none of the same values. We also look at Adam, and how he decides what to believe and which facts are trustworthy.

FOLLOW UP QUESTIONS

1. Think about Anathema and her relationship to Agnes's prophecies, including how she studies and uses them in her life. Do you see parallels with your relationship with the Bible?
2. If you're part of a faith community, look at its statements of belief, or one of the established Creeds.

a) What do these statements mean to you? If you're reading this as part of a group, do others in your group interpret them in the same way?
b) Do your community's statements of belief provide guidance on how to act? If not, does your organisation also have a set of values? Do these values align with your own?

WATCH: AZIRAPHALE AND THE ANGELS
(Episode 4, 40:31 – 42:18)

After rejecting Crowley's offer to escape in favour of staying and trying to stop Armageddon, Aziraphale is accosted in Soho by the archangels Michael, Uriel and Sandalphon. Michael threatens him; as far as they're concerned, it's 'time to choose sides'. Aziraphale, backed up against a wall on a bustling London street, tries to assert himself. Sides are important, he tells them, because humans have to make choices about their values. Angels, though, should keep the world spinning so that humans can keep doing that. Uriel tells Aziraphale he thinks too much, as Sandalphon punches him in the gut. Aziraphale seems hurt and shocked: 'Why would you do this? We're the good guys.' Aziraphale tells them he will report their behaviour to 'a higher authority,' but he's too late, they are summoned away and the others leave to take their places in the heavenly army.

PROMPT QUESTIONS

1. Aziraphale has long been suggesting to Heaven that they seek an alternative to war and the end of the world. Why don't the angels want to hear what he has to say?
2. In Episode 3, when Aziraphale challenges the need for a war, Uriel tells Gabriel, 'that's an angel that's been down there too long.' Has Aziraphale been polluted by the influence of 'the world' in the pejorative sense, or have his experiences on Earth given him a positive ability to empathise and therefore broaden his views?
3. Think about your morals, values, beliefs and the things you care about. Have these things ever changed? Why?

GOING DEEPER
Alex reflects:
Aziraphale doesn't deny the reality of God, Satan, Heaven, Hell, or all the hosts thereof. He knows Jesus personally. He believes God has a plan and he's diligent in following it to the best of his ability, even when (e.g. at the Flood or the Cross) he's doubting God's methods.

Why, then, is it so hard for him to fit in with the other angels? Don't they believe the same things? Aren't they working towards the same goal? It becomes apparent throughout the show that they aren't.

Aziraphale's crisis is not one of faith but of values. The people he works with (his family, his community, his nation, his church) have a very different moral framework to his own. Communication between the two is ineffective, as we see in the clip. They're either not listening to each other, or not hearing each other.

What possible parallels could we draw between this and our own personal and global cultural conflicts?

'You're ridiculous,' says Uriel, dismissive, contemptuous, and pleased to fight a war Aziraphale doesn't want.

'Time to choose a side,' warns Michael.

Aziraphale has a very strong sense that this is not what angels should be. He is deeply troubled. 'Why would you do this? We're the good guys,' he pleads.

I feel for Aziraphale. I spent a long time in a former church community, attempting to work within the structure and respect authority while advocating change to no effect. I was baffled for years. We all agreed that the church was intended to do good, so I didn't understand why those who led the congregation were being so intractable when confronted with injustice. Why did we prevent the participation of openly LGBTQ+ members of the congregation in worship? Why did we speak so excitedly about multinational corporate ventures without also highlighting how many of them rely on slave labour and cause active harm to the environment? Why was it so important to reinforce the idea that women love shopping and men love guns? Weren't we supposed to be the good guys?

I was very frustrated. In the midst of this, I came across a way of framing this experience that really helped me. There's a sociological model called Moral Foundations Theory[1] that describes a person or a society's values on several sliding scales, like contrast or brightness controls on a computer screen. They describe what somebody cares about.

Beliefs: We Believe

The sliders are:

- Care vs. Harm (e.g. being driven by compassion and other's interests, versus prioritising self-interest no matter the outcome for others).
- Fairness vs. Cheating (Both relating to how you'll behave to achieve your goals. Do you insist on only working with options that are available to everyone, or do you use every tool in your kit no matter what?)
- Loyalty vs. Betrayal (i.e. to the group identity. Would you ever be prepared to act against your nation's desires or interests? In what situation? Perhaps your group identity doesn't influence your choices at all and you could switch sides and stab your old allies in the back with little remorse?)
- Respect for authority vs. desire for subversion of authority. (Do you walk on the grass even though the sign forbids it, or do you avoid the grass just in case even when there's no sign?)
- Sanctity vs. Degradation, (i.e. concern for purity of the group identity, or a monoculture, where sameness is valued, versus valuing variety, diversity, and the blurring of boundaries.)
- Liberty vs. Oppression (i.e. choice vs. control).

The model isn't perfect; it's just one of several sociological tools for studying morality, but I found it helpful when I didn't seem to be able to get through to my church leaders about the issues that mattered to me, and I didn't understand why that might be.

In particular, thinking about the sanctity/degradation slider helped me process conversations I had when England and Wales legalised same-sex marriage in 2013. Many in the congregation at the time lamented that this devalued their own heterosexual marriages: marriage – so important to their own identity and faith – all of a sudden also encompassed something they considered to be wrong.

Other friends jeered this point of view by asking me if

these concerned couples were aware gay marriage 'wouldn't be compulsory' – no one was going to *make* anyone marry someone of the same sex! So why did it matter? To them, this was no one else's beeswax.

These reactions come from opposite ends of this sliding scale of values. For those who value 'sanctity' in this sense, the inclusion of something they disapprove of, within something they're part of, degrades something powerfully sacred. For those who value inclusion, this point of view doesn't make sense, because as far as they're concerned boundaries are personal, arbitrary and malleable: of course, marriage should be open to all.

I've had a stab at placing Aziraphale, Crowley and Gabriel on these sliding scales – what do you think?

Aziraphale can only work with Gabriel as long as he, Aziraphale, suppresses his instinct to care for humanity in the interests of angelic ambition, denies his connection with Crowley to preserve Heaven's sanctity, and demonstrates his loyalty to the group. Aziraphale and Crowley work well together because their shared causes of care and liberty matter more to them than their differences. They share a moral framework in all the ways they consider most important.

I eventually realised my discomfort with my former church wasn't that they and I believed different things (although we did), but that we didn't agree on what was best for people and the world. That was hard, but something I eventually found very releasing. It made me realise we were fundamentally incompatible. Unequally yoked (2 Corinthians 6:14), like Aziraphale and Heaven, this community and I were never going to be able to work together long term.

I have strong opinions about what's right and wrong, but I don't think there's anything about our moral conflicts that is a surprise to the Divine. Perhaps that was what Jesus was getting at when he said, 'I have not come to bring peace, but a sword.' (Matthew 10:34). And even as we acknowledge there are times when we have to part ways with people, we also have Jesus' reminder that, 'If you love those who love you, what reward will you get? Are not even the tax collectors doing that?' (Matthew 5:46)

These questions are big! And they're contentious. And they're important. We have to decide how we proceed when faced with difference: after all, it's our reality.

FOLLOW UP QUESTIONS

1. Although the other angels view Aziraphale with suspicion, we're given the impression that if he had kept his mouth shut and toed the party line, he'd have been allowed to remain working with Heaven for eternity. What might that have cost him? What might that have cost the world?

2. If you're in a community (faith, workplace, family, or other) with different values to yours, do you feel as if you belong? Are there any conditions you have to meet in order to fit in? If so, can you imagine what might you be freed up to do if you didn't have to expend energy to perform in this way?

3. If you're in a community where you do feel like you belong, how do you support those who exist on the margins, or are having to work harder, change, or hide in order to participate? Are there ways in which you can share or relieve that burden?

4. I ended up leaving the church I mentioned, but that's not to say we can't be called to participate in communities and organisations we're in conflict with. Have you been in a similar situation? How do you decide whether to stay or go? Where do you draw the line?

WATCH: ADAM AND THE WORD
Episode 3: 37:05 – 39:04, Episode 4 (0:00 – 2:15)

Anathema tells Adam about her powers, her profession, and her concern for the planet. Adam agrees global ecological tragedies are awful – though his biggest problem with nuclear power stations is that they make for a boring school trip. Anathema gives Adam magazines for further reading, though instead of ecology these contain sensationalist articles with mythological content. Adam soaks the articles up like a sponge. At the beginning of Episode 4, his friend Pepper is sceptical: she doesn't think the sunken city of Atlantis or alien messengers are real. Adam dismisses her challenge: 'Things on the internet can be made up,' he tells her. 'This is magazines.'

STARTING QUESTIONS

Adam thinks the internet can contain falsehood, but that to publish something untrue wouldn't be allowed! What do you think?

1. Think about how you access information (e.g. published books, television programmes, online video content, social media, internet comment threads, heart-to-heart conversations with friends in the pub). Explore the reasons you might trust some more than others.
2. Where do you go to find out what's happening in the world day to day? Do you know anything about the values of the people or systems that provide it? Can you identify the biases those sources of information have?
3. Think about the Bible. Could you get different ideas about what God values from reading, say, Ezra chapter 9 as opposed to the book of Ruth? How about the actions of the Levite in Judges 19 to 21 versus Jesus' words from the Sermon on the Mount?

GOING DEEPER

When we were teenagers in the late 1990s and 2000's, UK government policy was to get half of school leavers into university. Opinion differed over whether this was a good thing, or if it would mean people who might otherwise have decided to develop their skills in more vocational ways would end up with qualifications that hindered rather than empowered them. It was popular to joke about young people going into 'useless' degrees like Media Studies: What do they do, watch screens all day? What possible good could come of studying television shows?

Twenty years later, in an era of ubiquitous images, near-limitless access to information, social media and 'fake news', training that equips us to interrogate the way we receive and process information through mass media is really useful!

Even digital natives aren't immune to making assumptions: Adam Young's take on the subject is that while you might not trust information on the internet, no one would be allowed to publish something in magazines that wasn't true. Oh, that sweet, summer child!

Jesus and the writers of the New Testament warn against being unwittingly influenced by the messages we receive (e.g. Matthew 23, Galatians 5:7–12, Romans 16:17–19, Jude, 1 Timothy 3–5). We are required to exercise great discernment and to interrogate our sources of advice and information. Who is telling us what; how are they pitching their stories? Why are they choosing to do so?

We don't have Adam Young's ability to instantly transport aliens across the galaxy, or divert shop owners from Tibet to dig tunnels under our landscape. Our imagination does shape the world we live in though, mostly by shaping ourselves. The media we absorb informs the reality we live in, often in subtle ways.

Media theorist Marshall McLuhan[2] coined the term 'the media is the message.' He argued that it's not just the *content* of the information, but *the way it's conveyed* that determines what we take from it. We see this in Episode 1 when Satan commandeers Crowley's car radio. He praises Crowley and says his work with the M25 was genius. On the other hand, the way Crowley's boss is choosing to communicate with him is intrusive, threatening, dangerous and doesn't respect his boundaries. Irrespective of the contents, the message *actually* tells Crowley that he's walking a tightrope over hellfire, that he's being watched, he's replaceable and that he should be afraid.

Similarly, well-meaning beautiful people on stage and screen can assure us that there's more to life than looks and fame – but if this is said by a person lit with a spotlight, or photographed tastefully in a magazine, we receive two messages. The individuals' words are probably really sincere, but the medium is saying something different! This unseen message not only makes a bigger impact on us than what is said, it can easily go unnoticed and become quietly internalised in our minds.

This implicit contradiction to the explicit words that we think we *ought* to believe gives us an uncomfortable itch in our souls that – left unidentified – can lead to cognitive dissonance: deeply ingrained inconsistent thoughts and beliefs that confuse and hinder our peace of mind. We end up saying things like, 'These things shouldn't bother me!' or 'I ought not care so much!' or 'I'm overthinking', while at the same time feeling miserable about it. This conflict can be the result of messages conveyed by a medium that contradicts the content.

Jesus tells us to exercise wisdom as we move through the world. When he speaks of some of the religious leaders he warns, 'Be careful to do everything they tell you. But do not do what they do, for they do not practice what they preach' (Matthew 23:3). In other words: pay attention to the medium as well as the message.

What we watch and listen to, as well as the company we keep, shapes our beliefs, our patterns of thought, our imaginations and consequently our actions. 'We become what we behold' as McLuhan put it. As people of faith, we have a responsibility to examine what it is we're becoming.

FOLLOW UP QUESTIONS

1. The Bible is full of stories, poetry, letters, songs, lists and other media. How do the different media in the Bible impact how you engage with the contents?

2. Recent authors like Rachel Held Evans[3] and Nick Page[4] share their own relationships with scripture. If you were to write a story about you and your relationship with the Bible, what genre would it be? Romance? Instruction manual? Misery memoir? Comedy? Tragedy? Action/ Adventure?

3. Is the Bible a source of authority for you? If so, in what way? N.T. Wright discusses this in a very readable essay available online if you're interested in a pragmatic scholarly perspective.[5]

4. We invited you earlier to think about the motivations and methodology of various media. Why do you think we wrote this book? What does it mean for how you react to what we've written?

CREATIVE REFLECTION
How to be relevant

> Cash flow
> Common sense
> Casual discrimination
> Christ.

Alex Booer, 2016

GET CREATIVE!
In the Beginning
Ephesians 1:4–10 presents a potted history of God's plan from start to finish. If you were to explain how you see the history of the universe in a paragraph, how would you do it? Where would you start? What would the end of the story be? What would happen in the middle?

Put the book down
We love the written word, but we're also big fans of making art and getting out of our heads by engaging our bodies. If you're not a fan of reading, what other media do you enjoy? Do you use them to explore your faith?

Glorious Tools
Alex works in civil engineering. Her colleague Jane once said, *'The Bible begins in a garden and ends in a city – and you can't*

get from one to the other without construction!' How does your life give you insight into God's plan and purposes that others without your experiences might not have?

Looking outward

How does what you believe and what you value impact your life? Perhaps you're a carer, or support a local food bank, encourage your friends, help out your neighbours, join your friends at the gym when they need motivation. Do you campaign for causes you care about? How is your faith and your worldview reflected in your deeds? How does that translate to your relationships, communities and politics? Balance up your thinking against the reminder that no one person or community can do everything; we all need each other.

CHAPTER FIVE

Hope: The Thing with Feathers

'Hope' is the thing with feathers –
That perches in the soul –
And sings the tune without the words –
And never stops – at all –
Emily Dickinson

A horse is a vain hope for deliverance;
despite all its great strength it cannot save.
Psalm 33:17

BIBLE READING
Job 17

STARTING ACTIVITY

Reflect on the Bible passage above using prompts below:

1. What word would you use to describe Job's feelings or attitude in this passage?
2. Can you think of a time in your life when your emotions reflected those of Job's? What enabled you to survive that time?

Prayer

> In the dark hours of the night,
> May we cling to the promise of morning.
> In the bitter cold of loneliness,
> May we stay close to the warmth of friendly hearts.
> When the weight of despair is heavy,
> May we cast our cares on He who is Strength.
> Amen.

TO START YOU THINKING

It is 1862 in St James's Park, London. Crowley and Aziraphale are feeding everything but ducks, and discussing what dire straits they may be in if heaven or earth were to find out about their agreement. If it were to all go 'pear-shaped,' as Crowley says. Aziraphale sighs and gazes with a melancholy air at the overfed geese and pigeons. 'I like pears,' he says. So often, finding hope in a seemingly hopeless situation is not a grand act, but a small one. A reflection on the joy of pears seems more than adequate.

The word 'hope' is found 129 times in the modern Bible. However, due to translation, the word we find is the translation of several Hebrew and Greek verbs. Some of these words are linked to trust and expectation, as the biblical writers put their 'hope' or 'trust' in God (Jeremiah 14:22), but also 'hope' for better circumstances that God might provide (Psalm 69:6, Psalm 22:5). In the cases of those writers of the book of Jeremiah and book of Psalms, often the hope is declared in order that better times may come and God will provide deliverance from terrible circumstances or surrounding enemies (Psalm 25:15, Psalm 27:14, Psalm 40:1). In the New Testament, hope becomes more of an eschatological concept as Paul encourages believers to focus on their hope for salvation (1 Th 5:8), eternal life (Titus 1:2) and resurrection (Acts 23:6). Hope, it seems, is a key theological concept for those who live inside the will of God. Yet, over and over again in the scriptures we encounter tales of those who are without hope. The people of God, those chosen and blessed, continue to suffer and languish in pain some without ever receiving the consolation they may have called for. The so-called 'Texts of Terror'[1] such as the oppression of Hagar, the rape of Tamar, the sacrifice of Jephthah's daughter give us horror stories of (mostly) women who are brutalised by their society without reprieve. Even when comfort or 'hope' might finally come as it does for a blessed few, it is often so little it could hardly be called hope: Hagar's only easement for a life of sexual slavery, physical abuse, and expulsion for death in the wilderness, is that her son will live (Genesis 21:14). It is hard not to see those words as yet a further erasure of Hagar and her painful experience – that there is no hope to be spared for her own life and future, only enough for her male child. When faced with the hopelessness of these painful lives, it is not difficult to understand why Job, in the midst of the desolation of his life, cried out: 'Where then is my hope? Who can see hope for me?'

We are taught in Sunday school that God is everlasting, and so the hope we have in him is similarly never-ending. As Emily Dickinson suggests, hope is the song that never stops singing. Yet, what can we do when we find ourselves in situations where we can draw no comfort from an expected hope, or a hope in the world to come as Paul suggests? What can we do when, like Job, we cannot find hope anywhere, or to use Dickinson's imagery, when the song of hope stops singing? There is no easy explanation. For some of the women we have mentioned, there is no consolation. For some of us living today, we may feel similarly afflicted by hopelessness. What we see in Aziraphale, however, is quite the opposite: he is afflicted with hope, perhaps too much of it, as he sometimes struggles to truly recognise the severity of his situation. His hope is drawn from the minutiae of human life: the ducks, the sushi, the pears he finds around him. Somehow, this does not trivialise the enormity of pain that we find in the world. This kind of hope does not offer to remove our wounds, rather it brings a beautiful poignancy to the littleness of daily objects – for there is a tragedy and a wonder to a world where millions of children like Hagar are enslaved in 2019 and yet nature continues to bring forth succulent, delicious pears.

In this chapter, we will be exploring this intriguing dichotomy of hope; how it survives, how it dies, how it can thrive even under inexplicably terrible circumstances. Our exploration will take us to the depths of Job's despairing cry but also to the precious joy of Aziraphale's pears. For somehow, in this world where we write new texts of terror every day, the song of hope, however faintly, still can be heard.

CREATIVE REFLECTION
The Hope of the world

The unseen hand pushes his small malleable head,
The heel of a holy palm forcing
Divinity out of her rage.
She strains, red veins emptying towards the source,
Shaking knees and hands tangled;

For the love of God, just pull
Him out, drag Him out,
Let it be finished!

From her stricken sex comes forth
Blood and water and God, gasping,
lizard-like eyes blinking in a wrinkled face.

The cord pulses.
He struggles plaintively against that unusual tethering
whilst his small lips and tongue first taste
salty sweat from her heaving navel,
her best gift.
It is too bitter for that holy Child,
who wails.

Emma Hinds, 2013

QUESTIONS
1. What does hope mean to you?
2. As Christians, what do we hope for?
3. Who or what do we place our hope in?

WATCH: AZIRAPHALE PETITIONS A HIGHER AUTHORITY
Aziraphale petitions the Metatron (Episode 4: 49:00 – 52:24)

Aziraphale attempts to contact the Almighty but instead gets through to The Metatron, 'The Voice Of God'. The Metatron assures him that 'to speak to me is to speak to God,' which is sort of true, but only in the sense of being a kind of politician's spokesperson. Aziraphale reiterates the information, context, plan, and hope that he's been conveying to Heaven's bureaucratic hierarchy since the antichrist was a child. He gets the same response he'd had from Gabriel and the other archangels: Good work, well done! However, irrelevant. There needs to be a war so Heaven can win it. We see Aziraphale's hope drain from his face. The authority he hoped would want peace is actually pro-war. Stiffening his resolve, Aziraphale goes to someone who hasn't let him down: he calls Crowley.

PROMPT QUESTIONS
1. Why is Aziraphale upset?
2. Do you think there's hope for the Metatron, Gabriel, Michael, Uriel and Sandalphon?
3. Do you think there's hope for the administrative system that makes up Heaven in the show? Are your answers to these two questions the same?
4. What happens to disappointed hope?

GOING DEEPER
Alex reflects:
'I don't for a moment think that's what the leadership intended,' is a common excuse for poor behaviour within a hierarchy. In any system that relies on tiers of authority to function, good intentions can be misheard, diluted or perverted. All this abuse wasn't the original goal; speak to the

higher-ups and they'll reassure you *they* meant well! Even if so, it's cold comfort for the people who are being hurt.

Aziraphale has spent 6000 years excusing Heaven. 'How can someone as clever as you be so stupid?' asks Crowley. What is Aziraphale hoping in? Is he right to hope?

Audre Lorde, who was (in her words) a 'Black, lesbian, mother, warrior, poet', and academic, spent her career addressing the convergence of racism, sexism, homophobia and class discrimination. She concluded that working within fundamentally unjust systems and hoping for transformation is unsustainable. 'The master's tools will never dismantle the master's house. They may allow us to temporarily to beat him at his own game, but they will never allow us to bring genuine change.'[2] As it is said, 'It is better to take refuge in the Lord than to trust in princes' (Psalm 118:9); princes don't have your best interests at heart.

Prior to our clip above, Aziraphale believes he can find someone within the institution who can listen to him and act accordingly, in love. Yet the further up he goes, he finds that Heaven is hawkish to the core: the warmongering is intentional. Aziraphale's trust in the establishment has brought – like the empire of Egypt to the Hebrews – 'neither help nor advantage, but only shame and disgrace,' (Isaiah 30:1–5). He isn't working for who he thought he was. In this moment we see him lose his career, source of support, 'birth' family, community, world-view, and hope all at once.

Ever had a relationship that you thought was forever, only for things to fall apart? Been betrayed or swindled by someone you trusted? Achieved a dream, only to realise the reality isn't the way you thought it would be? You understood the world one way, and it turns out you were wrong. The rug is pulled from under you and suddenly you're off balance and falling.

What did you do when the thing you put your hope in let you down?

What Aziraphale does is run to the one person who can

understand where he's coming from. 'Without community,' says Lorde, 'there is no liberation, only the most vulnerable and temporary armistice between an individual and her oppression.' Aziraphale drops his loyalty to his employer and he takes up his own power, gleefully embraces the courage of his convictions, goes off to find Crowley and helps save the world. It's great telly.

I wonder, though if this is an accurate reflection of what happens immediately after we experience a loss this momentous. When your life has collapsed around you, burned to the ground in charcoal and ash, what do you do? Our lives aren't a story that needs to wrap up in six one-hour episodes.

Survival, says Audre Lorde, 'is learning how to stand alone, unpopular and sometimes reviled, and how to make common cause with those others identified outside the structures in order to define and see a world in which we can all flourish. It is learning how to take our differences and make them strengths' (Lorde, 1979).

Learning takes time. When we're disappointed, we need to learn how to survive our loss. We need to grieve.

Aziraphale's story reminds me of Megan Phelps-Roper, who grew up in the Westboro Baptist Church and whose memoir[3] charts her change of mind and subsequent departure from that organisation and her family.

I'm also reminded, inevitably, of my own recovery which was, and still is, messy! I called it my Angry Church Divorce. I had questions and regrets: Was any of it ever real? Was I stupid to stay for so long and make it work? I've wasted so much time/money/life! What do I do now?

There's a cost to emancipation. I found wisdom and comfort in the testimonies of others who'd been there before me (Rohr, Bessey, Held Evans, Bolz-Weber, Dobson, Narloch & Williamson[4]) but I also experienced crippling anxiety, palpitations, and a panic disorder. I couldn't face approaching anything spiritual or emotional for a long time. I needed to heal before I moved on.

In the midst of this process, I met with a friend who had no frame of reference for my experience. 'If you don't have faith anymore, what do you believe?' she asked, confused. I told her I believed that I wouldn't always be where I found myself in that moment and that this wasn't the end of my relationship with faith. That a church institution had disappointed me, but the mystery of God wasn't something I was done with.

Audre Lorde claimed that powerful structures can't be redeemed, and said that this notion 'is only threatening to those [women] who still define the master's house as their only source of support.' Aziraphale survives because he is able to accept the truth of this, to step outside the 'house' and still hope that – perhaps – God's plan transcends the plans of the ethereal machine. He has moved from trusting a system to trusting in a mystery.

If you're disappointed, you're not alone. You're walking in the footsteps of the psalmists, the prophets and those who came before us. Unless the seed dies it remains a seed. We, like Aziraphale, trust not in horses, chariots, churches, or our employers, but in possibility, the ineffable name of the Lord, and a universe that hasn't run out of surprises.

FOLLOW UP QUESTIONS

1. Heaven – Aziraphale's 'master's house' – isn't his only source of support. He has someone to go to, he isn't alone. But when our lives fall apart, we may also lose our support structures. What alternative support might you seek for yourself or provide for others when change is unavoidable? (We realise for many, choosing to leave situations can be dangerous.)

2. Brunhilde Pomsel[5] (1911–2017) worked for years as a secretary to Josef Goebbels, the Nazi Minister for

Propaganda, and was imprisoned for it after the war. She lived a quiet life and seems to have otherwise been a nice person. Her testimony (Pomsel & Hansen, 2018) is fascinating. What very real and understandable pressures do we face which can mean we follow the herd or the institution, or stay in relationships that we know confine us and others?

3. How does your inner life, your personal morality, spirituality and holiness, contribute to your hope and the hope of the world?

WATCH: CROWLEY GIVES UP
Crowley mourns his best friend (Episode 5: 11:15 - 13:40)

Crowley is drunk in a pub, already two bottles of spirits down, and ordering another. He's trolleyed. He believes Aziraphale to be not just discorporated but permanently destroyed. Crowley laments his Fall, blaming his decision to side with Lucifer on boredom and mild discontent. His grief is interrupted when Aziraphale appears in front of him, fuzzy around the edges. Crowley's so drunk he's not sure if he's seeing things: no, he didn't go to Alpha Centauri alone, he lost his best friend and he's abandoned running away in favour of getting drunk and waiting for the world to end. He even took a souvenir from the bookshop, a reminder that he could hold at the last. Happily, he picked a good book.

PROMPT QUESTIONS

1. Crowley's had to face lifelong consequences of a decision he made when he was younger. Do you live with the outcomes of actions you regret? What does hope mean to you in this context?

2. Think about the stories of the saints, lives of historical figures, stories of people in the Bible, or people in

your own life. How has God used the constraints of irreversible circumstances to bring hope and possibility? Does that change how you feel about your own circumstances?

GOING DEEPER

Crowley's last words to Aziraphale's face end up being, 'when I'm off in the stars I won't even think about you!' Talk about regrets!

Crowley believes Aziraphale to be gone forever, and with him has gone Crowley's hope for the future. Of course we know Aziraphale is fine. Hang on in there, Crowley! He'll be along in a minute! Lo and behold, this scene ends with Aziraphale on Earth, indisposed but alive, and with Crowley restored to purpose, direction, sarcasm and – maybe – hope.

Well, lucky them.

Most of us who suffer loss don't get our people back.

The book of Ruth tells the story of Naomi, whose husband and sons have died. She will never see them again and she has no means to support herself or her daughters-in-law. Like Crowley, her hope for the future is gone and she sees herself as rejected by God.

> 'Even if I thought there was still hope for me—even if I had a husband tonight and then gave birth to sons— would you wait until they grew up? Would you remain unmarried for them? No, my daughters. It is more bitter for me than for you, because the Lord's hand has turned against me!' (Ruth 1:12–13).

Having lost everything, Naomi has decided to return to the town she was born and to die there. Naomi means 'pleasant,' but when she arrives back in Bethlehem she can't bear to be confronted with even her own name.

Hope: The Thing with Feathers

'Don't call me Naomi,' she told them. 'Call me Mara, because the Almighty has made my life very bitter. I went away full, but the Lord has brought me back empty. Why call me Naomi? The Lord has afflicted me; the Almighty has brought misfortune upon me.' (Ruth 1:20–21)

How do we even start to talk about hope in the presence of grief? What do we know of hope when grief grips us and thrusts us, naked, every nerve fully exposed, to the chilling and inescapable reality of loss? Grief can't be controlled. To be in its grip is to stand constantly on a precipice that at any moment may choose to collapse and swallow us whole. Hope? That's not just rude, it's painful.

For those with faith in an afterlife, it's perhaps tempting to fast-forward to hope when we lose people. We can offer encouragement that we'll see our loved ones again in Heaven, and reassure ourselves that this isn't the end of our relationships. It's okay! They're happy and with God! It might be easy to convince ourselves we don't need to grieve and can go straight to rejoicing. But if, like Naomi, we have lost someone we'll never see again in this life, it doesn't mean we shouldn't be sad. Confronted with the reality of Lazarus' death, even Jesus wept (John 11:35). Lazarus is raised by Jesus' own command, mere moments later, yet Jesus was moved to tears. Hope isn't a reason not to mourn.

'Blessed are those who mourn, for they will be comforted,' says Jesus in Matthew 5:4. Grief happens to us. We may defer it, or ignore it, or repress it, but it will find its way out somehow. Mourning is a doing word. Mourning demands that we stop, and feel, and surrender to the process of grief. Perhaps it is how we take up our lives again; to accept that we are here, and they are not, and there's nothing we can do about it. This is heart-breaking and hard.

Naomi doesn't get her sons or her husband back. Her future isn't without hope, though – it just takes a form she'd never anticipated. Ruth has a son, and 'Then Naomi took the child in her arms and cared for him. The women living there said, "Naomi has a son!" And they named him Obed. He was the father of Jesse, the father of David.' (Ruth 4:16–17) Naomi, in her grief and the circumstances of her loss, becomes part of Jesus' family tree.

Crowley does get his friend back, but he can never undo his fall from grace. Crowley's reality is that he has been irrevocably changed. He's no longer an angel but because he's not an angel, he has a role in the world that still needs saving.

We've all lost things we had to leave in the past. Whether we are mourning people, pets, possibilities, relationships, old hopes, beliefs, or abilities we had in our youth, we have no choice but to move on without them. Crowley's 'thing with feathers' interrupts him when he least expects it. Perhaps we can hope for the divine to interrupt us too.

FOLLOW UP QUESTIONS

1. Aziraphale is able to meet Crowley in the pub because he uses his imagination to make connections others haven't. How does our imagination expand our capacity for hope? Whose imagination has inspired you to hope?

2. In Episode 6, when Newt is confronted with the lie that is his preferred reality, he has to be brave. He has to let go of what he wishes reality to be ('I'm a computer engineer!') and embrace what is ('Every time I touch a computer it breaks') in order to bring hope to a desperate situation. How might embracing an uncomfortable reality enable you to imagine hope or possibility you might not have otherwise seen?

3. What is it you hope for?

GET CREATIVE!

Beautiful nebula

Crowley helped make at least one nebula. He *helped*; he wasn't alone. Was he working with other angels, or was this a shared project between the Almighty and one of her curious children? What was that like? Was it like making glitter pictures with your toddlers, or recruiting your children into helping you build a garden shed? If you want to, you could imagine it! Maybe you could make star pictures with your kids, or visit an observatory. Or get happy with some glitter – you're never too old!

Tell me a story

Children are the world's hope for a better future! What do the Them do with their lives? Where are they when they reunite in 20 years' time? What happens to Warlock? Does he ever get to say goodbye to his Nanny and the gardener?

Do panic?

Speaking of children, Greta Thunberg, addressing the Global Economic Forum on 25 January 2019, said:

> *Adults keep saying:* 'We owe it to the young people to give them hope.' *But I don't want your hope. I don't want you to be hopeful. I want you to panic. I want you to feel the fear I feel every day. And then I want you to act. I want you to act as you would in a crisis. I want you to act as if our house is on fire. Because it is.*

What do you hope for? Are you waiting to act on that hope? Is there anything that you're hoping someone else will do that perhaps you're in a position to do yourself? Perhaps you are where you are precisely for such a time as this (Esther 4:14).

The Sound of Music
In addition to Queen and Shakespeare, *Good Omens* fandom seems to have adopted Richard Siken, Mary Oliver, Emily Dickinson, and Hozier as their poet laureates in inspiring moods and soundtracks to their stories. What songs or poems do you associate with your favourite fictional characters?

CHAPTER SIX

Love and Renewal: These Remain

'Certainly there was an Eden on this unhappy earth. We all long for it, and we are constantly glimpsing it: our whole nature at its best and least corrupted, its gentlest and most humane, is still soaked with the sense of "exile".'
J. R. R. Tolkien

'The kingdom of heaven is like a mustard seed, which a man took and planted in his field. Though it is the smallest of all seeds, yet when it grows, it is the largest of garden plants and becomes a tree, so that the birds come and perch in its branches.'
Matthew 13:31–32

BIBLE READING
Isaiah 43:16–21 (KJV)

Thus saith the Lord, which maketh a way in the sea, and
    a path in the mighty waters;
Which bringeth forth the chariot and horse, the army
    and the power; they shall lie down together, they
    shall not rise: they are extinct, they are quenched as
    tow.
Remember ye not the former things, neither consider
    the things of old.
Behold, I will do a new thing; now it shall spring forth;
    shall ye not know it? I will even make a way in the
    wilderness, and rivers in the desert.
The beast of the field shall honour me, the dragons and
    the owls:
    because I give waters in the wilderness, and rivers in
    the desert, to give drink to my people, my chosen.
This people have I formed for myself; they shall shew
    forth my praise.

STARTING ACTIVITY

Take a look at the above bible verse as it is written in the King
James Version. Compare it to a different biblical translation
that you might have at home. What do you notice about the
difference in phrasing? Does it change anything about how
you understand the passage?

Prayer

God almighty,

Give us ears to hear the whispers of Spirit
Let us smell and taste the bittersweet Kingdom fruit.
Give us touch to feel the brushing closeness of the next world coming,
And eyes to see, where we can, the edges of angel wings.

Amen.

TO START YOU THINKING

Words matter

Did you know that the word 'dragon' appears numerous times in the King James Version of the bible? A word that has sadly been lost from more modern translations due to an emphasis on scientific accuracy. In today's life of worldwide information, we balk at such elaborations in language. If our vicar or bishop or preacher told us 'here be dragons,' we would reach our inquisitive fingers towards our phones to consult the ever present encyclopaedia of the internet. For us, multiple sources and voices are accessible at the tap of a screen or the push of a computer key: discussion, facts, evidence, we can gather them all ourselves. We can become experts without ever having to leave our pew.

Yet imagine instead, that you are a churchgoer in 1611. Perhaps you are a teenager or a young apprentice in a small village in rural Derbyshire. You have learnt to read a little for your trade, have been Sunday school taught, but books are not part of your daily life. You do not travel beyond the bounds of your village, you will work in it, marry in it, raise a family in it and die in it without seeing places less than ten miles away. On Sunday, when you attend church, the vicar reads the passage from Isaiah, or perhaps from Psalm 91, or the book of Job and you hear the word: *dragon*. In your mind's eye images are brought together from the meagre resources you have; a local boy who told you dragons had fangs, the stained glass window of Saint George that shows them to be squirming, snakey creatures, and the biblical narratives that have taught you they are fearsome beasts. You know they are not English creatures, but you imagine them curled in fire or wreathed in smoke in some faraway country. No one could tell you that the word 'dragon' is a derivation of ancient French and Latin for large serpent and was likely linguistically developed to understand discoveries of unexplainable fossils, when the idea of the dinosaurs were still a blink in the scientific eye. There was no evidence to dispute you. There, in a tiny Derbyshire church, a dragon is conjured, through the power of the imagination.

It would be silliness to suggest that we should be longing for a less educated, scientific time so that we may be able to believe in dragons once more. Our history, at least to the human eye, only moves in one direction: forward. However, there is a yearning for imagination in the human condition that cannot be denied and will not be denied. In a world where the vast sharing of 'fact' through the information highway, we actually find ourselves in the midst of a million and one fictions masquerading as facts. If the rise of 'fake news' has taught us anything, it's that our appetite for a tall tale has only grown with our capacity to absorb information. There is always someone we might scoff at for the fantasy of their beliefs – 'Oh, they believe in conspiracy theories, they're so ignorant' – and perhaps willingly accepting a narrative in which a super-race of lizard people secretly runs the world and then deciding to share it widely on the internet displays a level of ignorance, but it also reveals the desire that is latent in all of us to create an imaginative reality. For really, as awe-inspiring as it is to know that the likes of the Tyrannosaurus rex once stalked our planet, would it not be as thrilling to imagine they also breathed fire and could fly? In a world where information is a dime a dozen, is it so shocking that millions of people world-wide are seeking a truth more elaborate or extraordinary than the one presented to them?

Especially when we might consider, as Christians who sometimes claim to be holders of an ultimate truth, that the truth we adhere to is so incredibly remarkable. As Christians, we routinely suggest people believe as fact what we might otherwise dismiss as fairy-tale. A God who sends angels and opens donkeys' mouths? A God-man who raises the dead and turns water to wine? A supernatural spirit that raised him and can empower believers? One has to ask if it would be much more of a stretch, truly, to throw some dragons in there. This is not to belittle the incredulity of Christianity's claims. It is rather to settle imagination where it truly belongs – within our faith as that which enchants and renews us. It is not to say that our beliefs are 'imagined' but rather, what we imagine are only shades of the great holy imagination that loves and renews us. What we believe about God is that he is wondrously unbelievable. That paradox needs to be embraced by us all.

In this chapter, we will be looking at the way 'enchantment' plays a role in renewal in Good Omens and the way forgiveness can exceed our imaginative capacities. We may even put a dragon in there, just for fun.

CREATIVE REFLECTION
Under the Pear Tree

Nobody could tell you how long the Mr Youngs had lived in Rosemead Gardens. Nobody recalled them and their ostentatious collection of houseplants and folios moving in, but everyone who lived on the square could tell you that the bench under the pear tree belonged to the Mr Youngs. The two gentlemen were often found there, one often eating a pear if they were in season or reading a book, the other smoking a cigarette, with his spare hand, and it's gold ring, resting gently on top of the hand of the man beside him.

Love and Renewal: These Remain

Mrs Beaton in number 6 was the only one who remembered the Mr Youngs from before they became the Mr Youngs, and remembered that they had not taken each other's strange and, in one case, unpronounceable names in civil union. When Mrs Beaton had asked why they had chosen 'Young' in particular, the red-haired Mr Young had said it wouldn't get old. The white-haired Mr Young had smiled and said it was simply a pleasant name.

For a long time it had seemed like the red-haired Mr Young might have had something, for they seemed unusually hale and hearty for men of questionable age. They had always laughed this away with jokes like 'pact with the devil,' or 'good genes,' or 'cod liver oil twice a day', but recently the children of Rosemead Square had noticed a change in the Mr Youngs. Red-haired Mr Young rarely shouted at them about their lack of musical knowledge or athletic skill, and white-haired Mr Young had taken to bringing a hot water bottle out to the bench when he read outside.

They could not know about the letter the Mr Youngs had received a few weeks ago. It had been a while since either of them had noticed any 'funny business,' decades even, but the letter had inexplicably turned up in the toast rack on Sunday morning. With the gold cresting, it was undoubtedly a letter from their old employer. After being opened with some trepidation, it turned out to be a perfunctory but not unpleasant missive: Time to get a move on. Well done, good and faithful servants.

The Mr Youngs were not surprised when the next day dawned and their previously mobile limbs were creaking. They merely smiled, took their time in shuffling to the coffee machine and got on with it. They bickered a little more about the effects of smoking on an ageing heart, and conversed a little more about whose turn it was to pick up the prescriptions. It was nearly time to move on. To where, they were not sure, the next step was quite ineffable, but they were assured they would be together.

On their bench, the not-so-red-haired Mr Young looked at the growing fruit above them.

'They're ripening.'
'Indeed.'
'Might get a taste before we go.'
'I do hope so.'

He squeezed his husband's hand. White-haired Mr Young looked up from his book.

'Happy?' asked Mr Young.
'Oh yes.'

Emma Hinds, 2019

WATCH: ON OUR OWN SIDE
On the bench (Episode 6: 24:43 – 28:21)

Aziraphale and Crowley wait for the bus. Crowley wonders if the Almighty had it planned this all from the start, while the International Delivery Driver – restored after a strange day – arrives to pick up the Horsemen's effects. 'Do you believe in life after death?' he asks Aziraphale, who acknowledges he must. The accoutrements of the apocalypse removed from between them, the angel and demon consider their next steps. No bookshop to go to: 'It burned down, remember?' 'You can stay at my place, if you like.' 'We're on our own side.' They're in trouble – they're going to have to choose their faces wisely. Crowley takes Aziraphale's hand as they sit next to each other on the bus. The next morning, the first day of the new world, God informs us, 'people who were dead were now alive, and things that were broken had now been miraculously restored.'

PROMPT QUESTIONS

1. Do you believe in life after death? In what ways is your belief important to you?
2. Aziraphale has made the decision to sever himself from Heaven, but in this clip he is still reticent to accept his new reality. Do you think Aziraphale forgives the angels? What's the difference between forgiveness and reconciliation? What are the risks we run if we conflate the two?

GOING DEEPER

In this scene, Crowley reiterates the pledge he made to Aziraphale at the bandstand in Battersea Park. 'We can run away together! We're on our own side!'

'I don't think my side would like that,' says Aziraphale.

Aziraphale! How do you still not get it?! 'Are you still so dull?' (Mark 7:18)

This is an angel who chose to trust God and openly defied Heaven's authority with sword in hand, yet here he is, turning back to look at the past he's left behind. He is still excusing himself to burying his father (Matthew 8:21), clinging to his riches (Mark 10:21–22), and worrying about his mother and brothers (Matthew 12:46–50). Jesus warns us about trying to force new wine into old wineskins (Luke 5: 36–38) and Aziraphale's still trying!

People got turned into pillars of salt for less, we're just saying.

We've said that we think time is required to adjust to big life changing decisions. Can we claim people need space to grieve and move on, and then expect Aziraphale to change the habits of 6000 years with a snap of the fingers? Is this what Jesus asks of us, if we're to follow him?

We see Aziraphale's arc reflected in that of Jesus' disciples. They too have an original puppy-like enthusiasm for their exclusive understanding of the coming Messiah's plan, hope for political change and moral superiority over the Gentiles. Who will be the greatest? Can I sit next to you when you're in charge? Isn't this temple fabulous! Who sinned, this man or his parents?

And then, the cross.

The tomb. The disappointment. The loss of everything they'd hoped for. The grief. They are adrift, until Sunday morning dawns with the man in the garden, an impossible surprise, a new plan, the road to Emmaus, reconciliation, a meal on the beach, a restoration of purpose. Their own side: not corporate loyalty but relationship, and a concern for all the earth (Acts 1:8).

More particularly, perhaps, we can draw parallels between Aziraphale and Peter, (Luke 22:54–62). They both take risks, but still instinctively protect themselves in the face of perceived threats. They take time to accept quite how many barriers God's love is prepared to break.

Peter's life-long process of learning and changing doesn't end with his restored relationship with Jesus. We accused Aziraphale with Jesus' words, 'Are you still so dull?' (Mark 7:18–19). When Jesus asks this of his disciples, Mark tells us it's in the context of Jesus declaring all foods clean. This isn't a revelation anyone had in Jesus' lifetime (though it's something Aziraphale, who loves his oysters, would no doubt appreciate!). It's Peter's revelation (recorded in Acts 10) when God, in Peter's dream, persuades him to kill and eat ritually unclean animals. 'Do not call anything impure that God has made clean.' (Acts 10:15) Peter argues that this goes against everything he's been taught is right but eventually, he realises God means it. Peter extends this metaphor to the context of a dilemma he's later faced with: does he accept that Gentiles can follow Jesus and receive the Holy Spirit too? Peter concludes that he can: 'I now realize how true it is that God does not show favouritism but accepts from every nation the one who fears him and does what is right.' (Acts 10:34–35).

Peter's visions suggest God's plan is always broadening in scope, something that necessarily requires mental adjustment for the people who thought they were safe on the inside of the existing boundaries. So, do we cut Aziraphale some slack?

When it comes to Aziraphale on the bench, and Peter at the fireside, Jesus suggests (Matthew 21:28–42) our instinctive response is not what counts, but the actions that follow it up. Faith, perhaps, like courage, involves being afraid, slightly in the dark, and doing the thing anyway. Aziraphale rejects Crowley with his words, but his actions – as we see later – are faithful to his decisions. Peter's developing understanding of God's purposes, and of right and wrong, is one that takes time, and changes with maturity. So perhaps we should cut Aziraphale a little slack. The Gospel and *Good Omens*' message of love that transcends expectations conquering all takes time to settle into our habits and minds. Discipleship is a life-long, uh, *discipline*. It's a road of repentance, even as we trust we're redeemed. We have the opportunity to screw up, turn around, trudge back, and hope we've learned enough in the process to do the whole thing faster next time.

This said, we still maintain Aziraphale has a lot of apologising to do ... Angel, you need to roll up your sleeves and put some work in because your friend there has zero self-esteem and he's moping. Get up to speed, you absolute flutter-brain.

FOLLOW UP QUESTIONS

1. 'Who are my mother and brothers?' asks Jesus. (Matthew 12:46) There's a strong theme of 'chosen family' woven through *Good Omens*: Aziraphale and Crowley, Anathema and Newt, Madame Tracy and Sgt Shadwell, even Adam, the Them and the Youngs. Why might these characters gravitate towards each other?

2. How does, or how might, your community take steps

to partner with, learn from and love people you might otherwise think are on opposing sides but who are looking to the same goals?

3. Christianity frequently embraces violence and imperialism to spread its influence. How do you understand Jesus' words in Acts 1:8 ('you will be my witnesses in Jerusalem, and in all Judea and Samaria, and to the ends of the earth') and does knowing that Judea and Samaria were 'hereditary enemies' change your thoughts about the passage?

WATCH: APPLES
Adam leaves the garden (Episode 6: 46:25 – 48:48).

Adam is confined to his parents' garden, leaving his friends to go to watch the circus set up without him. He's not allowed out for years and years – or tomorrow at the earliest. Of course, if Dog were to escape, Adam would have to go after him. Adam's powers allow Dog a route out of the garden and, token objection made, Adam races out into the fields. God tells us the summer is coming to an end; something is ending that can never be re-lived. Adam steals an apple – he can't see what the fuss is about. 'There never was an apple that wasn't worth the trouble you got into for eating it.'

PROMPT QUESTIONS
1. 'You can't just refuse to be what you are,' says Gabriel, to Adam, in Episode 6. Is that what Adam's doing?
2. God's words in this scene tie the story back to the apple in the first garden. Can you identify recurring themes or threads that run through your own life?
3. Childhood – with its lack of personal admin and relatively low responsibility! – can be a time of great imagination and deep thoughts. What are the things you remember thinking deeply about as a child?

GOING DEEPER

'All that matters is to be one with the living God
to be a creature in the house of the God of Life.
Like a cat asleep on a chair
at peace, in peace…'

Pax – D. H. Lawrence

The journey of the saving of the world is drawing to a close – Adam has restored Aziraphale to his bookshop and Crowley to his car, Anathema and Newt are on their path to marital bliss, the armies of heaven and hell have retreated and Adam has his father back. Why then, should there be a sense of melancholy pervasive in the moment when Adam gleefully flees his back garden to follow Dog on further adventures? God says:

'Something told him that something was coming to end. Not the world, exactly, just the summer. There would be other summers, but there would never be one like this. Not ever again.'

We might wonder: Is that really a bad thing? After all, Adam's summer has been full of darkness and pain and the appearance of the literal embodiment of Satan. That's enough to give anyone nightmares. Why then, should there be a sense of mourning? It is perhaps not because Adam will miss the darkness of his dreams, or the spontaneous appearance of Death but that perhaps he will miss a way of seeing the world that has been previously open to him but shall now be closed. Adam may keep some of his powers, for instance, the power to make trees dissolve so he can escape his garden, but he will grow and become more human with time. The magic of his summer, of being a child with a child's self-belief and a child's view of the universe, will fade. With that, comes a peculiar homesickness, a sense of melancholy that Alison Milbank calls, 'this feeling of homesickness for the truth'.[1]

As children, we have a particular and curious way of seeing the world. What we believe can be disconnected from reality and yet be more real to us than anything else. Consider when

Adam and his friends play a game of witch hunts. For them, they accept the reality they have imaginatively created. Just consider the way Adam and his friends are able to defeat the four horsemen by saying what they 'believe'. For them, belief is not disconnected from reality. Belief is fact. For adults, this ability to transform the world with our words and thoughts is something we might feel homesick for, something we may catch glimpses of again in the moments when we question reality. Alison Milbank describes how, 'Getting up in the night as an adult can give one this same rush of reality: new sounds and creaks, objects that might move at any moment. Even our pet cat encountered in the dark is a mysterious new creature.'[1] The natural path of growth, the path that Adam and his friends must now go down that we all go down as we grow and mature and leave the garden, leads away from a constant state of imaginative reality. Yet, that does not mean it cannot be returned to.

J. R. R. Tolkien believed that the process of imagination, of engaging in fantasy, could be a theological exercise. In his essay, On Fairy Stories,[2] he wrote about how there could be a 'recovery' of sorts when considering our imaginative capacity. It is not only an escape but a way to return to what we have lost: to see the world anew again, awash with enchantment or perhaps, enchanted once again by the Holy Spirit. Adam and his friends will never have the same summer again, one in which the veil between earth and the supernatural was pierced and divine magic showed up all around them, or burst up from the ground of an airstrip. Yet, if they continue to pay attention, to keep their eyes and ears open and their minds open to imaginative possibilities, they might still 'recover' moments of insight into the extraordinary.

FOLLOW UP QUESTIONS

1. 'Anyone who will not receive the kingdom of God like a little child will never enter it.' (Mark 10:15). What does this mean to you?
2. There is a rich tradition of mysticism present throughout the history of Christianity. Have you ever experienced a glimpse into the extraordinary?
3. How do you keep your metaphorical eyes and ears open to moments of meaning and connection, in your relationships with family, friends and the divine? Do you adopt any particular habits or practices?

GET CREATIVE

Good and Faithful Servant

What on earth does Lesley the Delivery Driver say to his wife Maud when he gets home?! Do your friends and family understand the ins and outs of your life when they're not around? Do you talk to them about school, or work, or your regular daily activities when you're together? Or do you just like to switch off?!

Story prompt – Good (W)omens

There aren't any on-screen friendships between women portrayed in this show. Perhaps you could imagine a friendship between two Chattering nuns, or Anathema and Mrs Young discussing life in Tadfield, or even Beelzebub and Dagon (not strictly women, but gender optional!) sharing their frustrations with Hell's infrastructure and administrative challenges.

Story prompt – Our Side

A Theory: Aziraphale needs to learn to love, and to see clearly, and to accept people as they are. Crowley needs to learn he's loved, and seen, and accepted as he is. What do they get up to with their lives after the failed apocalypse?

Yelling at the plants

Fan lore has it that Crowley terrorises his plants as a way of externalising his own trauma from the Fall: he's playing the part of an angry god who casts out and destroys those who fail to meet his exacting standards![3] Do you like to garden? Does your creativity manifest in lawns, geometric borders, and the colours and textures that change with the seasons? Perhaps you grow apple trees, or have an allotment, or even a windowsill. Celebrate that in whatever way you like, even if that's shouting at it to grow better!

Please tweet us with pictures of your most 'encouraged' plants!

Afterword

We really hope you've enjoyed this book, and that it's got you thinking about the *Good Omens* TV show and your own faith from different perspectives. We had a lot of fun putting it together.

We've shared some of our final thoughts below!

So, who's your favourite character?
Emma: Pepper. She doesn't tolerate mansplaining!

Alex: True. Cheek! Mine might be Deirdre Young. I love her. She doesn't have many lines but Sian Brook portrays her beautifully. We get this sense Deirdre knows she has custody of something bigger than her understanding, just like any other parent who's ever thought, 'I wonder what on earth is going on in their head?' She looks like she thinks Adam's inner world is something precious and to be protected, while accepting it could grow into something she can't control.

Who would you cosplay as?
Alex: I want Anathema's coat. Or Madame Tracy's. Strong coat-game. Also, the Archangel Michael's floaty shirt.

Emma: Crowley as Nanny Ashtoreth, because I already have the skirt. And I love the lullaby she sings, I'd like to sing that creepily to people at Halloween.

Alex: She's so beautiful.

What didn't you fit into the book?

Alex: There's so much we didn't get to talk about! I had a whole section called 'Apocalypse Nope' about placing the book of Revelation in its historical and geographical context, but it would have been cribbed entirely from Nick Page's Bryson-esque travel-theology memoire *Revelation Road* so everyone who's interested should just go read that instead.

I was also talking with a friend who sees a transgender narrative in Crowley's thoughts about his identity – all that brooding over his Fall! Crowley's colleagues are all well suited to their demon-ness, but Crowley is always turning it over and over, and acting against the template he 'ought' to follow as a demon. They compared Crowley's laments to the common quip that 'people who are cis-gender don't interrogate their gender to this extent' – but with being a demon instead of being trans. Crowley, you sweet disaster-area! It's okay! You don't have to be either/or, you can just be yourself and save the world. Also, that angelic noodle you hang out with needs you, because you're several steps ahead of him on the same journey and he'll get there eventually.

Emma: I could have written all day about the post-apocalyptic shenanigans of the four horsemen. I love the Pratchett-Gaiman imagining of them – I want them to have their own show!

Is there anything you think is sinister about this show?

Emma: Nope! I don't think there's anything to be afraid of here.

Alex: Not in itself, but I think it shows how dangerous it can be when organisations or people with power are challenged. Look at how Heaven treats Aziraphale, or the fate of Sister Theresa Garrulous: 'We speak what is on our minds!' she says, outraged at being told to shut up, only to be promptly murdered. Hastur is the worst.

If you were going to get creative and make something based on the show, what would you make?
Alex: We already made this book.

Emma: I'd always go to writing. Or embroidered samplers with quotes, I like those. I feel like an embroidery of a trembling cactus with 'GROW BETTER!' on it would look great next to my more disobedient house plants.

Alex: Felt art! I was planning to make a felt picture of Aziraphale and Crowley flying in space in front of a nebula. Felt's a great medium for skies. And I do write a lot of fan-fiction!

What do you hope people get out of this book?
Emma: How much value there is in imaginatively approaching theology through literature. There's depth available when we engage with culture and see what it can bring us rather than being frightened of it.

Alex: I like that. I hope people use the creative prompts too, because I love seeing what people make of things. I want to see what our readers see in *Good Omens* that we might not have done and find out how other people experience the world and the divine. Tell us your stories!

If you want to share your thoughts or creative endeavours, you can find us on Twitter @IneffablyLovely

Appendix: Welcoming Non-Binary People and Using They/Them Pronouns

This was originally written by our friend Lois Stone for the St Nicholas Burnage church magazine in November 2018. They've kindly allowed us to use it here! It provides some context and guidance – along with further resources – for helping make non-binary people welcome in church. Lois is a non-binary person whose doctoral research focused on the representation of trans people in museums and popular media. Lois prompted a discussion of Crowley presenting as a woman at the cross, which started us off on the process of writing this book!

'Non-binary' is an umbrella term and means that a person does not identify as either a man or a woman. There are lots of different ways non-binary people define their own gender. Some people might identify as both male and female, some might identify as somewhere between male and female, and some might identify as neither male nor female. All are valid. Many people have not met a non-binary person before, so here are some helpful tips when speaking to or about non-binary people:

Many, but not all, non-binary people use the singular

'they' pronoun instead of 'he' or 'she'. The singular 'they' has been a part of the English language since 1375, but it can still feel awkward to use if you're not used to it. The best thing to do is to practise. For example, after talking to a non-binary person you could practise by thinking to yourself, 'It was so nice to see them at church. I'm glad they had a good week.'

Sometimes you might use the wrong pronoun. It happens! The best thing to do is to correct yourself and continue what you were saying. For example, you might say 'I was talking to him, sorry, them, about volunteering at our next event.' Over-apologising brings more attention to the mistake and can make the person you're speaking about feel awkward. Over-apologising also pressures them to comfort you about your mistake, when the situation is about making sure that they feel safe and comfortable.

If you hear someone else use the incorrect pronoun for a non-binary person, it is best to politely correct them. For example, you can wait for the person to finish their sentence and then respond, 'They use "they", actually' or 'Sorry, you said "she" but that person uses "they".' As a non-binary person it can be exhausting to repeatedly correct other people when they use the wrong pronoun, and someone else correcting the mistake lets the non-binary person know that they are being actively accepted by your group or community.

If you're not sure about someone's pronoun, it is usually ok to politely ask.

Keeping the last point in mind, coming out can be very intimidating for non-binary and trans people, especially in church settings. If you are meeting someone for the first time and are not sure about their pronoun, best practice is to let them know what your pronouns are. For example, you might say 'Is this your first time joining us for worship? Welcome! I'm Mary and I use she/her pronouns.' Telling someone your pronouns lets them know they are in a safe place where they can be themselves, and invites them to also share their pronouns if they feel comfortable to do so.

If you are interested in learning more about non-binary people and about how to make your church a welcoming and affirming place for trans people, these resources are a good place to start:

- *Life Isn't Binary: On Being Both, Beyond, and In-Between* by Meg-John Barker and Alex Iantaffi
- *This is my body: Hearing the theology of transgender Christians* by Christina Beardsley and Michelle O'Brien
- *Trans Affirming Churches: How to Celebrate Gender-Variant People and Their Loved Ones* by Christina Beardsley and Chris Dowd
- *Transfaith: A Transgender Pastoral Resource* by Chris Dowd and Christina Beardsley
- *Transforming: The Bible and the Lives of Transgender Christians* by Austen Hartke.

Notes

INTRODUCTION

1. Afterword to the US edition of *Good Omens*
2. 'Creative works about characters or settings created by fans of the original work, rather than by the original creators'
3. https://archivesofourown.org/works/19730593 accessed 17 August 2019
4. https://twitter.com/neilhimself/status/11504289784754 09408?lang=en
5. See a useful glossary of terms by the Proud Trust at https://www.the-proudtrust.org/resources/resource-downloads/glossary/

CHAPTER ONE: JUSTICE: LIKE A RIVER

1. The prayer here references names of people who died by violence in or before 2019. Since then, other names have been brought to global attention: Ahmaud Arbery, George Floyd, Breonna Taylor, Sarah Everard… We join those who protest the injustices that perpetuate this violence. We still cry: justice.
2. Sarah Bessey, *Out of Sorts: Making Peace with an Evolving Faith* (Darton, Longman and Todd, 2015)
3. Richard Dawkins, *The God Delusion* (Bantam Press, 2006).
4. Greg Boyd, *The Crucifixion Of The Warrior God* (Fortress Press, 2017).

CHAPTER TWO: BODY AND MATTER: SOME BODY TO LOVE

1. Tom Wright, *Creation, Power and Truth: The Gospel in an Age of Cultural Confusion* (SPCK, 2013).
2. Paula Gooder, *Heaven* (SPCK, 2011); Paula Gooder, *Body* (SPCK, 2016).
3. Rachel Mann, *Dazzling Darkness: Gender, Sexuality, Illness and God* (Wild Goose Publications, 2012).
4. Nadia Bolz-Weber, *Shameless: A Sexual Reformation* (Canterbury Press, 2019).

5. Glennon Doyle, *Love Warrior* (Thorndike Press, 2016).
6. Jamie Lee Finch, *You Are Your Own: Reckoning with the Religious Trauma of Evangelical Christianity* (Amazon, 2019).
7. C. S. Lewis, *Mere Christianity* (1952).
8. Tom Wright, *1 Corinthians For Everyone* (SPCK, 2013).

CHAPTER THREE: POWER: I GAVE IT AWAY!

1. Sabrina Flanagan, *Hildegard of Bingen: A Visionary Life*, 2nd Edition (Routledge, 1998); Fiona Maddox, *Hildegard of Bingen: The Woman of her Age* (Headline Book Publishing, 2001).
2. Ibid.
3. Twitter, 10 July 2019

CHAPTER FOUR: BELIEFS: WE BELIEVE

1. Jonathan Haidt, *The Righteous Mind: Why Good People are Divided by Politics and Religion* (Penguin Random House, 2012).
2. Marshall McLuhan, *Understanding Media: The Extensions of Man* (1964).
3. Rachel Held Evans, *Inspired: Slaying Giants, Walking on Water, and Loving the Bible Again* (Nelson Books, 2018).
4. Nick Page, *The Badly Behaved Bible: Thinking again about the story of Scripture* (Hodder & Stoughton, 2019).
5. https://ntwrightpage.com/2016/07/12/how-can-the-bible-be-authoritative/

CHAPTER FIVE: HOPE: THE THING WITH FEATHERS

1. Term first coined by Professor Phyllis Trible in her ground-breaking 1984 exegesis and feminist criticism, *Texts of Terror*.
2. Audre Lorde, essay: *The Master's Tools Will Never Dismantle The Master's House* (1979), published in *Your Silence Will Not Protect You* (Silver Press, 2017).
3. Megan Phelps Roper, *Unfollow: A journey from hatred to hope* (Farrar, Straus and Giroux/Riverrun 2019)
4. Richard Rohr, *Falling Upward: A Spirituality for the Two Halves of Life* (SPCK, 2012); Sarah Bessey, *Out of Sorts: Making Peace with an Evolving Faith* (Darton, Longman and Todd, 2015); Rachel Held Evans, *Searching for Sunday: Loving, Leaving, and Finding the Church* (Thomas Nelson, 2015); Nadia Bolz-Weber, *Cranky, Beautiful Faith: For irregular (and regular) people* (Canterbury Press, 2013); Kent Dobson, *Bitten by a Camel: Leaving Church, Finding God* (Fortress Press, 2017); John Williamson and Adam Narloch, The Deconstructionist Podcast, https://thedeconstructionists.com

5. Brunhilde Pomsel, Thore D. Hansen (translated by Shaun Whiteside), *The Work I Did: A Memoir of the Secretary to Goebbels* (Bloomsbury Publishing, 2018).

CHAPTER SIX: LOVE AND RENEWAL: THESE REMAIN

1. Alison Millbank, *Apologetics and the Imagination: Making Strange in Imaginative Apologetics – Theology, Philosophy and the Catholic Tradition*, Ed. Andrew Davison (SCM, 2011).
2. J.R.R. Tolkein, *On Fairy Stories* (HarperCollins, 2014, essay originally published 1947).